JESUS

12 QUESTIONS THAT COULD CHANGE YOUR LIFE

Gene Keith
October 2018

What do you know about Jesus? Do you believe in the Mormon Jesus? What about the Jehovah's Witness Jesus? Or perhaps you believe in the Muslim Jesus? Each group preaches a different Jesus. Can they all be right? Who was Jesus? Someone said *He is either a liar, a lunatic, or the Son of God?* What do you say?

We thank you for taking the time to read this book and we are praying that you will follow the example of C.S. Lewis, who after spending many years as a skeptic, changed his mind and became a devout follower of the Lord Jesus Christ.

Forward

Who is Jesus? Where did he come from? There are so many different ideas being circulated today, including the idea that Jesus never actually existed. What do you believe? I personally agree with the statement made by the late Oxford scholar C.S. Lewis in his book, "Mere Christianity."

"A man who was merely a man and said the sort of things Jesus said wouldn't be a great moral teacher. He would either be a lunatic on the level of a man who says he's a poached egg - - or else he would be the devil of hell; you must take your choice.

Either this was and is the Son of God, or else a mad man or something worse.

You can shut Him up for a demon or you can fall at his feet and call Him Lord and God. But don't come up with any patronizing nonsense about Him being a great moral teacher. He hasn't left that alternative open to us."

C.S. Lewis

Table of Contents

Chapter 1

Who is This Person Called Jesus?

It is frightening to learn how little this present generation knows about God, Jesus, and the Bible. A survey revealed that fewer than half of all adults could even name the four gospels. Many Christians cannot identify more than two or three of the disciples. 60% of Americans can't name even five of the Ten Commandments. 82% of Americans believe, "God helps those who help themselves," is a Bible verse.

Those identified as born-again Christians did better by one percent. 50% thought that Sodom and Gomorrah were husband and wife. A considerable number of respondents indicated that the Sermon on the Mount was preached by Billy Graham. We are in big trouble.

What Difference Does It Make?

We may not know about Sodom and Gomorrah or be able to name any of the disciples or any of the Ten Commandments, but we dare not enter eternity and not know who Jesus is and what He did when He came to earth and died on the cross.

What do you know about Jesus? Who is He? Was Jesus merely a great religious leader? Was Jesus merely a great teacher?

Do you believe in the Mormon Jesus? What about the Jehovah's Witness Jesus? Or perhaps you believe in the Muslim Jesus? Each group preaches a different Jesus. Can they all be right? Who was Jesus? Someone said *He is either a liar, a lunatic, or the Son of God?* What do you say?

Testimony of an Oxford Scholar

Years ago, an Oxford University scholar and agnostic named C. S. Lewis spent many years denying the Deity of Christ. But after years of serious research and searching for answers, he yielded his life to Jesus Christ and became a devout follower of our Savior. One of his books was titled "Mere Christianity" and I love what he said about Jesus.

"A man who was merely a man and said the sort of things Jesus said wouldn't be a great moral teacher. He would either be a lunatic on the level of a man who says he's a poached egg - - or else he would be the devil of hell; you must take your choice. Either this was and is the Son of God, or else a mad man or something worse. You can shut Him up for a demon or you can fall at his feet and call Him Lord and God. But don't come up with any patronizing nonsense about Him being a great moral teacher. He hasn't left that alternative open to us."

Wow! This is something to think about. The author said it was patronizing nonsense to call Jesus a great moral teacher. Jesus is either who He said He was, or a liar, a demon, or worse. The former skeptic said we must make our choice. What is your choice? Was Jesus who He said He was? Who did He say He was? What does the Bible say about Jesus?

Was Jesus God in the Flesh?

(Isaiah 9:6) "For unto us a child is born, unto us a Son is given: and the government shall be upon his shoulder, and his name shall be called "Wonderful, Counselor, The mighty God, The everlasting Father, The Prince of Peace."

Was Jesus Equal with God?

(Phil. 2:5-7) Let this mind be in you, which was also in Christ Jesus: Who, being in the form of God, thought it not robbery to be equal with God: But made himself of no reputation, and took upon him the form of a servant, and was made in the likeness of men.

Was Jesus the Son of the Living God?

In Matthew 16, Jesus asked His disciples, "Who do people believe I am? Peter said he believed Jesus was THE CHRIST, the Son of the living God. Jesus was pleased with that answer and told Peter that God Himself had revealed that fact to him (Matt. 16:13-17)

13 When Jesus came into the coasts of Caesarea Philippi, he asked his disciples, saying, whom do men say that I the Son of man am?

14 And they said, some say that thou art John the Baptist: some, Elias; and others, Jeremiah, or one of the prophets.

15 He saith unto them, but whom say ye that I am?

16 And Simon Peter answered and said, Thou art the Christ, the Son of the living God.

17 And Jesus answered and said unto him, Blessed art thou, Simon Barjona: for flesh and blood hath not revealed it unto thee, but my Father which is in heaven.

Show us the Father

The disciples one day told Jesus that they would be satisfied if He would show them God, the Father. Jesus told them flatly that those who have seen Him (Jesus) had seen the father (John 14:8-9).

[8] Philip saith unto him, Lord, show us the Father, and it sufficeth us.

[9] Jesus saith unto him, Have I been so long time with you, and yet hast thou not known me, **Philip? he that hath seen me hath seen the Father;** and how sayest thou then, Show us the Father?

God in the Flesh

(John 1:1-14) In the beginning was the Word, and the Word was with God, and the Word was God.

[2] The same was in the beginning with God.

[3] **All things were made by him; and without him was not anything made that was made.**

[4] In him was life; and the life was the light of men.

[5] And the light shineth in darkness; and the darkness comprehended it not.

[6] There was a man sent from God, whose name was John.

[7] The same came for a witness, to bear witness of the Light, that all men through him might believe.

[8] He was not that Light but was sent to bear witness of that Light.

[9] That was the true Light, which lighteth every man that cometh into the world.

[10] He was in the world, and the world was made by him, and the world knew him not.

¹¹ He came unto his own, and his own received him not.

¹² But as many as received him, to them gave He power to become the sons of God, even to them that believe on his name:

¹³ Which were born, not of blood, nor of the will of the flesh, nor of the will of man, but of God.

¹⁴ And the Word was made flesh, and dwelt among us, (and we beheld his glory, the glory as of the only begotten of the Father,) full of grace and truth.

Was Jesus the Creator?

(Col. 1:13-17)¹³ Who hath delivered us from the power of darkness, and hath translated us into the kingdom of his dear Son:

¹⁴ In whom we have redemption through his blood, even the forgiveness of sins:

¹⁵ Who is the image of the invisible God, the firstborn of every creature:

¹⁶ **For by him were all things created, that are in heaven, and that are in earth, visible and invisible, whether they be thrones, or dominions, or principalities, or powers: all things were created by him, and for him:**

¹⁷ And he is before all things, and by him all things consist.

Did Jesus Have the Power to Forgive Sin?

(Matt. 9:2-7) ² And, behold, they brought to him a man sick of the palsy, lying on a bed: and Jesus seeing their faith said unto the sick of the palsy; **Son, be of good cheer; thy sins be forgiven thee**.

³ And, behold, certain of the scribes said within themselves, This man blasphemeth.

⁴ And Jesus knowing their thoughts said, wherefore think ye evil in your hearts?

⁵ For whether is easier, to say, **thy sins be forgiven thee**; or to say, Arise, and walk?

⁶ But that ye may know that the Son of man hath power on earth to forgive sins, (then saith he to the sick of the palsy,) Arise, take up thy bed, and go unto thine house.

⁷ And he arose and departed to his house.

Was Jesus Worshiped by Angels?

(Heb. 1:1-6) God, who at sundry times and in divers manners spake in time past unto the fathers by the prophets,

² Hath in these last days spoken unto us by his Son, whom he hath appointed heir of all things, **by whom also he made the worlds**;

³ Who being the brightness of his glory, and the express image of his person, and upholding all things by the word of his power, when he had by himself purged our sins, sat down on the right hand of the Majesty on high:

⁴ **Being made so much better than the angels**, as he hath by inheritance obtained a more excellent name than they.

⁵ For unto which of the angels said he at any time, thou art my Son, this day have I begotten thee? And again, I will be to him a Father, and he shall be to me a Son?

⁶ And again, when he bringeth in the first begotten into the world, he saith, **and let all the angels of God worship him.**

Every Knee Shall Bow to Jesus

One day, every person who has ever lived, will bow down before Jesus and confess that He is Lord (Phil. 2:6-11).

⁶ Who, being in the form of God, thought it not robbery to be equal with God:

⁷ But made himself of no reputation, and took upon him the form of a servant, and was made in the likeness of men:

⁸ And being found in fashion as a man, he humbled himself, and became obedient unto death, even the death of the cross.

⁹ Wherefore God also hath highly exalted him, and given him a name which is above every name:

¹⁰ That at the name of Jesus every knee should bow, of things in heaven, and things in earth, and things under the earth;

¹¹ And that every tongue should confess that Jesus Christ is Lord, to the glory of God the Father.

Who is Jesus? Is He a liar? Is He a Lunatic? Or is Jesus the Son of God?

Jesus is Now Serving as High Priest

(Hebrews 4:14-16) "That is why we have a great High Priest who has gone to heaven, Jesus the Son of God. Let us cling to him and never stop trusting him.

This High Priest of ours understands our weaknesses, for he faced all the same temptations we do, yet he did not sin. So, let us come boldly to the throne of our gracious God. There we will receive his mercy, and we will find grace to help us when we need it."

Jesus is Serving as our Advocate

(1 John 2:1-2) "My little children, these things write I unto you, that ye sin not. And if any man sin, we have an advocate with the Father, Jesus Christ the righteous:

2 And he is the propitiation for our sins: and not for ours only, but also for the sins of the whole world."

What is an Advocate? Jesus our advocate is our supporter. Jesus has our back. Jesus is our promoter. Jesus is our activist. Jesus is our sponsor. Jesus is our campaigner. Jesus is our encourager. This is what Jesus is doing in heaven for you right now!!!

Jesus is Preparing a Place for Us

(John 14:1-3) Let not your heart be troubled: ye believe in God, believe also in me.

[2] In my Father's house are many mansions: if it were not so, I would have told you. I go to prepare a place for you.

[3] And if I go and prepare a place for you, I will come again, and receive you unto myself; that where I am, there ye may be also.

Jesus is The Only Way to Heaven

(John 14:4-6) And whither I go ye know, and the way ye know.

[5] Thomas saith unto him, Lord, we know not whither thou goest; and how can we know the way?

[6] Jesus saith unto him, I am the way, the truth, and the life: no man cometh unto the Father, but by me

Summary

Please don't take the attitude Hillary had on Benghazi, when she said: *"At this point, what difference does it make?"*

It makes a lot of difference. It makes the difference between heaven and hell. We dare not enter eternity and not know who Jesus is and what He did when He came to earth and died on the cross.

Jesus said, "If you believe not that I am He, you will die in your sins."(John 8:24b)

Chapter 2

Was Jesus Really Born of a Virgin?

In this chapter, we want to answer at least six specific questions. Was Mary really a virgin? Why is the Virgin Birth so important? Did Mary maintain her virginity after Jesus was born? Can Mary really help us when we pray? Is it proper to refer to Mary as the "Mother of God?" First, let's read what the Bible has to say on this controversial subject.

What does the Bible Teach?

(Matthew 1:18-25) 18 This is how Jesus the Messiah was born. His mother, Mary, was <u>engaged to be married</u> to Joseph. But before the marriage took place<u>, while she was still a virgin, she became pregnant</u> through the power of the Holy Spirit.

19 Joseph, her fiancé, was a good man and did not want to disgrace her publicly, so he decided to break the engagement quietly.

20 As he considered this, an angel of the Lord appeared to him in a dream. "Joseph, son of David," the angel said, "do not be afraid to take Mary as your wife. For the child within her was conceived by the Holy Spirit.

21 And she will have a son, and you are to name him Jesus, for he will save his people from their sins."

22 All of this occurred to fulfill the Lord's message through his prophet:

23 "Look! The virgin will conceive a child! She will give birth to a son, and they will call him Immanuel, which means 'God is with us.'"

24 When Joseph woke up, he did as the angel of the Lord commanded and took Mary as his wife.

25 But he did not have sexual relations with her until her son was born. And Joseph named him Jesus."

A Great Controversy

There was a great controversy back in 1950's over the meaning of the word translated "virgin" in Isaiah 7:14. Liberals insisted that the word translated "virgin" simply meant a young woman (not necessarily a virgin).

It's sad to say, but the worst critics of the virgin birth are not the atheist or the agnostics. In my opinion, the worst critics of the virgin birth are the infidel preachers who stand in pulpits of liberal churches and those wolves in sheep's clothing who teach in some theological seminaries, who deny the virgin birth.

Rumor about Mary

We know Mary was pregnant before she got married and one of the rumors was that the baby was the child of a Roman soldier named Panthera, who was stationed in Nazareth. A church leader named Origen (185-254) mentions this myth. What is your opinion? Was Mary really a virgin?

Did Mary remain a virgin after Jesus was born?

Were Jesus' brothers and sisters Joseph's children from another marriage? The official position of the Roman Catholic Church is that Jesus' mother, Mary, remained a virgin for her entire life. What is your opinion?

The Mother of God?

Roman Catholics speak of Mary as the "Mother of God." This was made official and incorporated in prayers at the third Ecumenical Council in Ephesus (Turkey) in AD 431. What is your opinion?

Free from Sin?

In 1854, Pope Pius IX declared that Mary was preserved from original sin. Catholics celebrate this Holy Day on December 8. What is your opinion?

The Glorious Assumption

In 1950 Pope Pius XII declared when Mary died, she was taken up, body and soul, to heaven. What do you believe?

Can Mary help us Pray?

How prominent is Mary in the Bible itself? All Christians acknowledge Mary as the virgin mother of Jesus Christ, but only Roman Catholics go so far as to elevate her to the position of mediator between believers and Christ Himself.

There are only five important references to Mary in the entire New Testament.

1. Luke 1:26-38

This is story of the visit of the angel Gabriel to Mary, announcing that she had been chosen by God to give birth to the promised Messiah.

26 Now in the sixth month the angel Gabriel was sent by God to a city of Galilee named Nazareth,

27 to a virgin betrothed to a man whose name was Joseph, of the house of David. The virgin's name was Mary.

28 And having come in, the angel said to her, "Rejoice, highly favored one, the Lord is with you; blessed are you among women!"

29 But when she saw him, she was troubled at his saying, and considered what manner of greeting this was.

30 Then the angel said to her, "Do not be afraid, Mary, for you have found favor with God.

31 And behold, you will conceive in your womb and bring forth a Son and shall call His name Jesus.

32 He will be great and will be called the Son of the Highest; and the Lord God will give Him the throne of His father David.

33 And He will reign over the house of Jacob forever, and of His kingdom there will be no end."

34 Then Mary said to the angel, "How can this be, since I do not know a man?"

35 And the angel answered and said to her, "The Holy Spirit will come upon you, and the power of the Highest will overshadow you; therefore, also, that Holy One who is to be born will be called the Son of God.

36 Now indeed, Elizabeth your relative has also conceived a son in her old age; and this is now the sixth month for her who was called barren.

37 For with God nothing will be impossible."

38 Then Mary said, "Behold the maidservant of the Lord! Let it be to me according to your word." And the angel departed from her."

2. Luke 2:15-19

This is the account of the angels appearing to the shepherds and instructing them to go to the stable in Bethlehem and find the Christ Child.

15 So it was, when the angels had gone away from them into heaven, that the shepherds said to one another, "Let us now go to Bethlehem and see this thing that has come to pass, which the Lord has made known to us."

16 And they came with haste and found Mary and Joseph, and the Babe lying in a manger.

17 Now when they had seen Him, they made widely known the saying which was told them concerning this Child.

18 And all those who heard it marveled at those things which were told them by the shepherds. 19 But Mary kept all these things and pondered them in her heart."

3. Matthew 12:46-50

This is the story of an encounter between Jesus and the messengers who had informed him that his mother and brothers were outside.

46 While He was still talking to the multitudes, behold, His mother and brothers stood outside, seeking to speak with Him.

47 Then one said to Him, "Look, your mother and your brothers are standing outside, seeking to speak with you."

48 But He answered and said to the one who told Him, "Who is My mother and who are My brothers?"

49 And He stretched out His hand toward His disciples and said, "Here are My mother and My brothers!

50 For whoever does the will of My Father in heaven is My brother and sister and mother."

Jesus' reply was not disrespectful, but at the same time, He made it clear that Mary had no more authority or influence on him than other ordinary disciples who believed in him and tried to obey him.

4. John 2:1-11

This reference to Mary is the only one that even remotely suggests that Mary had any "pull" with Jesus. In this situation, Mary told Jesus that the host had run out of wine. He told her that his time had not yet come. Nevertheless, she told the servants to do whatever Jesus told them to do. They did, and Jesus performed his first miracle.

"1 On the third day there was a wedding in Cana of Galilee, and the mother of Jesus was there.

2 Now both Jesus and His disciples were invited to the wedding.

3 And when they ran out of wine, the mother of Jesus said to Him, "They have no wine."

4 Jesus said to her, "Woman, what does your concern have to do with Me? My hour has not yet come."

5 His mother said to the servants, "Whatever He says to you, do it."

6 Now there were set there six water pots of stone, according to the manner of purification of the Jews, containing twenty or thirty gallons apiece.

7 Jesus said to them, "Fill the water pots with water." And they filled them up to the brim."

8 And he saith unto them, Draw out now, and bear unto the governor of the feast. And they bare it.

9 When the ruler of the feast had tasted the water that was made wine and knew not whence it was: (but the servants which drew the water knew;) the governor of the feast called the bridegroom.

10 And saith unto him, every man at the beginning doth set forth good wine; and when men have well drunk, then that which is worse: but thou hast kept the good wine until now.

11 This beginning of miracles did Jesus in Cana of Galilee and manifested forth his glory; and his disciples believed on him.

5. John 19:25-27

This is the last reference to Mary and Jesus in the New Testament. While dying on the cross, Jesus entrusted the care of his mother Mary to his disciple John. And that's the end of it.

25 Now there stood by the cross of Jesus His mother, and His mother's sister, Mary the wife of Clopas, and Mary Magdalene.

26 When Jesus therefore saw His mother, and the disciple whom He loved standing by, He said to His mother, "Woman, behold your son!"

27 Then He said to the disciple, "Behold your mother!" And from that hour that disciple took her to his own home."

There is nothing in the Bible to even suggest that Mary was to be exalted. Mary was a virgin when Jesus was born but did not maintain her virginity after Jesus was born.

Mary should not be called "The mother of God."

Mary was not born without sin nor did she live without sin.

When Mary died, her body was not taken up into heaven.

Mary can't help us when we pray.

Virgin means virgin

The word used there is used seven other times in the Old Testament and each time it is translated "virgin."

The Septuagint, translated from Hebrew into Greek 200 years before Christ, used the word "parthenos," and translated it "virgin."

The King James English revision in 1881 translated it "virgin."

The American Standard Version in 1901 translated it "virgin."

In Matthew 1:23, when the angel translated it for Joseph, he translated it "virgin."

Our church's Statement of Faith clearly spells out our belief in the Virgin birth of Jesus Christ. Every officer, every teacher, and every volunteer are required to believe in the virgin birth.

Why is the virgin birth important? It is important because if Jesus was the natural born son of Joseph and Mary, He cannot be our Savior, nor is He qualified to sit on David's Throne and reign as King.

We inherit our sinful nature from our fathers

The Bible teaches that every man, woman, and child are born with a sinful nature. Do you realize where that sinful nature came from? We did not inherit our sinful natures from our mothers.

We inherit our sinful natures from our fathers. A child is formed in the womb of a mother when the sperm (seed) of the man unites with the egg of the mother.
The seed comes from the man. Paul said in (Rom. 5:12), "Wherefore, as by one-man sin entered into the world and death by sin, and so death has passed upon all men, for that all have sinned."

Jesus was the seed of the woman (Genesis 3:15)

The Bible is clear on the fact that the "seed" (Jesus) would come from a woman.

If Jesus was the natural born son of Joseph, He cannot be our Savior. So, God came up with a plan whereby He could send a sinless person to die for the sins of sinful people. That person was Jesus.

Jesus was the Lamb without blemish

God taught this concept to the Jewish people in the system of sacrifices set up in the Old Testament. Animals brought to the temple for sacrifices had to be perfect and "without blemish." When Jesus came to John the Baptist to be baptized in the River Jordan, John pointed to Him and said, "Behold, the Lamb of God who taketh away the sin of the world."

Jesus will one day reign as King over all the earth

The virgin birth is also important, for without it, Jesus would not be qualified to be the King and reign on David's Throne.

Joseph was a descendant of King David

The purpose of those genealogies in Matthew and Luke were put there to prove to the Jews and Gentiles alike that Jesus was the heir to the throne of David.

Both Joseph and Mary are in the royal family of David. However, there was a problem in the line of Joseph. Just before the captivity, there was a king named "Jeconiah." There was a curse on his line and if Jesus were the son of Joseph, He could not serve as King.

Mary was also a descendant of King David

Mary was also a descendant of King David. And since the king could not come through the royal line, the king could come through the legal line.

Jeconiah and Coniah are the same person. Jeconiah sinned and God judged his family by not allowing any of his descendants to sit on the throne and rule as kings.

If Jesus had been the son of Joseph, He could not be Savior. God sent Jesus through Mary instead of Joseph so that Jesus could legally be heir to the throne of David.

Summary

1. The Bible teaches clearly that Jesus was the virgin-born son of Mary. The Holy Spirit impregnated the Virgin Mary when she was espoused (legally engaged) to Joseph.

2. Both Joseph and Mary were descendants of King David. However, there was a curse on Joseph's line making it impossible for Jesus to someday reign on David's throne if He had been the natural son of Joseph.

3. Mary was also in the Royal line and there was no curse on her side. In addition to that, if Jesus had been the natural son of Joseph, He could not be our Savior because He would have inherited a sinful nature from his father, Joseph.

4. The "seed" comes from the father, not the mother. But since Jesus was born from the "seed of a woman" (See Genesis 3:15), Jesus can be both our Savior and our coming King.

Chapter 3

Was Jesus Really Born on Christmas?

(Matthew 2:1-18)

Now when Jesus was born in Bethlehem in Judea, **during the reign of King Herod**. About that time some wise men from eastern lands arrived in Jerusalem, asking,

2 "Where is the newborn king of the Jews? We saw his star as it rose, and we have come to worship him."

3 **King Herod** was deeply disturbed when he heard this, as was everyone in Jerusalem.

4 He called a meeting of the leading priests and teachers of religious law and asked, "Where is the Messiah supposed to be born?"

5 "In Bethlehem in Judea," they said, "for this is what the prophet wrote: 6 'And you, O Bethlehem in the land of Judah, are not least among the ruling cities of Judah, for a ruler will come from you who will be the shepherd for my people Israel."

7 Then Herod called for a private meeting with the wise men, and he learned from them the time when the star first appeared.

8 Then he told them, "Go to Bethlehem and search carefully for the child. And when you find him, come back and tell me so that I can go and worship him, too!"

9 After this interview the wise men went their way. And the star they had seen in the east guided them to Bethlehem. It went ahead of them and stopped over the place where the child was.

10 When they saw the star, they were filled with joy!

11 They entered the house and saw the child with his mother, Mary, and they bowed down and worshiped him. Then they opened their treasure chests and gave him gifts of gold, frankincense, and myrrh.

12 When it was time to leave, they returned to their own country by another route, for God had warned them in a dream not to return to Herod.

13 After the wise men were gone, an angel of the Lord appeared to Joseph in a dream. "Get up! Flee to Egypt with the child and his mother," the angel said. "Stay there until I tell you to return, because Herod is going to search for the child to kill him."

14 That night Joseph left for Egypt with the child and Mary, his mother,

15 **and they stayed there until Herod's death**. This fulfilled what the Lord had spoken through the prophet: "I called my Son out of Egypt."

16 Herod was furious when he realized that the wise men had outwitted him. He sent soldiers to kill all the boys in and around Bethlehem who were two years old and under, based on the wise men's report of the star's first appearance.

17 Herod's brutal action fulfilled what God had spoken through the prophet Jeremiah:

18 A cry was heard in Ramah, weeping and great mourning. Rachel weeps for her children, refusing to be comforted, for they are dead.

Herod Was King

Matthew begins by stating the Jesus was born in the days of Herod the King.

The first time you admit to your professor that you believe the Bible he will remind you that Herod died in 4 BC, which was three years before Christ was born.

Your professor is right, but what the professor is not telling you is that the calendar we use is wrong. The fact is, Jesus was really born in 6 or 5 BC, probably in October, but not December.

The First Term of Cyrenius

The second thing we notice from the Bible is that Jesus was born when Cyrenius was Governor of Syria (Luke 2:1-3).

And it came to pass in those days, that there went out a decree from Caesar Augustus, that all the world should be taxed. (And this taxing was first made when Cyrenius was governor of Syria).

Luke, who was a medical doctor, states that Jesus was born when Cyrenius was Governor of Syria (Luke 2:2).

Be on guard here. Skeptics will try to undermine your faith by informing you that Cyrenius ruled over Syria *after Jesus was born*.

This is true. But ask your skeptic if he/she is aware that *Cyrenius served two terms*. He served one term before Christ was born and he served another term after Christ was born. Tell your professor that the Bible (Doctor Luke) made it clear that the census was taken during Cyrenius' *first term in office*.

Not December 25

The fact is, Jesus was not born on December 25. In fact, He was not even born in December.

When Jesus was born, the shepherds were still out in the fields with their flocks. They would probably have been indoors if it had been wintertime.

Also, it does not seem practical for Joseph to take his pregnant wife on a long journey, on the back of a donkey, in the dead of winter.

Summary

Celebrating the birth of Christ on December 25 is simply a tradition. In our opinion, there is no harm in this, as long as we don't place tradition on the same level as the Word of God.

We believe Jesus was born in 6 or 5 BC and probably around October. The fact is, He WAS born, He is alive, and He is coming back soon.

Chapter 4

Was Jesus Really Crucified on Friday?

The Good Friday Tradition

All our lives, most of us have been taught that Jesus died on Friday. We call it "Good Friday." However, there's a major problem with that. There is no way Jesus could have been crucified on Friday and fulfilled the prophecy given in Matthew 12.

I had never given much thought to this question until I came across a sermon by the late Dr. John R. Rice in which he pointed out that Jesus had been crucified on Wednesday. After reading that sermon and doing some research, I concluded that Good Friday is a tradition that cannot possibly be supported by Scripture.

Why is the day important?

1. We believe the day is important for three reasons. The first reason the day is important is because we want our family, our friends, and the members of our church to know and believe the truth.

Jesus said, *"Ye shall know the truth and the truth shall set you free."* If "Good Friday" is simply a tradition or a myth, we want to be the first ones to know about it.

2. Second: The day of the crucifixion is important because I personally believe "Good Friday" is a myth based on tradition, and Jesus accused the religious leaders of His day of *"making the Word of God of none effect by your traditions."* In other words, those religious leaders put their own man-made ideas ahead of the inspired Word of God. We must never base doctrine on anything that is not true.

3. Finally, the day of the crucifixion is important when we are dealing with skeptics.

The Bible says we are to be always ready to tell people what we believe and why we believe it (I Peter 3:15) "Instead, you must worship Christ as Lord of your life. And if someone asks about your Christian hope, always be ready to explain it." (NLT).

Skeptics are forever trying to find fault with the Bible, and there is no way Jesus could be crucified on Friday, remain in the grave for three days and three nights, and be resurrected on Sunday. We don't need to waste any precious time defending something that the Bible does not teach.

What we believe

We believe Jesus rode into Jerusalem on the tenth day of the month (Jewish calendar).

He, like Passover lambs, was observed from the tenth through the fourteenth day of the month.

He was crucified in the afternoon of the fourteenth day of the month, which was the same day the Passover lambs were slain, and their blood smeared on the doorposts of the homes.

Jesus was in the tomb for three days and three whole nights, fulfilling the only "sign" Jesus was willing to give, which was the "sign of Jonah."

Sometime before daylight on Sunday, the 17th day of the month, Jesus came out of the tomb, alive and well.

For the next forty days, Jesus showed Himself alive on ten different occasions. He appeared after His resurrection to individuals and to groups. One of those appearances was to a group of more than five hundred people, most of whom were still alive when Paul wrote the first letter to the church in Corinth (I Corinthians 15).

Jesus was in the tomb three whole days and three whole nights (Matthew 12:38-40).

When the religious leaders demanded that Jesus give them a "sign" to prove He was who He claimed to be, He said that the only sign He would give them was the "sign of Jonah." Read what He said and try to understand the significance of this "sign." For those who claim to be Christians yet look upon the stories of the Bible as allegorical, let us remind you that Jesus took those stories literally.

Jesus believed in creation.

Jesus believed in Adam and Eve.

Jesus believed in Noah and the flood.

Jesus believed the story of Jonah and the great fish (we assume it was a whale).

Consider also that the miracle of Jonah is not that Jonah remained alive in the belly of the whale for three days and three nights. The miracle is that he died in the belly of the whale. He was dead three days and three nights and God brought him back to life and sent him on to Nineveh to preach.

(Matthew 12:38-40) 38 Then some of the scribes and Pharisees answered, saying, Teacher, we want to see a sign from you.

39 But He answered and said to them, "An evil and adulterous generation seeks after a sign, and no sign will be given to it except the sign of the prophet Jonah.

40 For as Jonah was three days and three nights in the belly of the great fish, so will the Son of Man be three days and three nights in the heart of the earth."

Jesus' enemies understood this

Jesus' enemies understood that He had predicted that He would be in the grave for three whole days (Matthew 27:62-66).

62. On the next day, which followed the Day of Preparation, the chief priests and Pharisees gathered together to Pilate,

63. saying, "Sir, we remember, while He was still alive, how that deceiver said, 'After three days I will rise.'

64. Therefore command that the tomb be made secure until the third day, lest His disciples come by night and steal Him away, and say to the people, 'He has risen from the dead.' So, the last deception will be worse than the first."

65. Pilate said to them, "You have a guard; go your way, make it as secure as you know how."

66. So they went and made the tomb secure, sealing the stone and setting the guard."

Jesus was in the tomb for three nights: Thursday night, Friday night, and Saturday night. He was in the tomb for three days: A portion of Thursday, all day Friday, and all-day Saturday.

Where did the idea of "Good Friday" come from?

The idea of Jesus being crucified on Good Friday probably came from assuming, that since Jesus was crucified on the day before the Sabbath, that Jesus must have been crucified on Friday, which was the day before the regular Sabbath which always came on Saturday.

A careful reading of John 19:31 will reveal the problem.

Look at this verse closely. John said that Jesus was crucified the day before the Sabbath and added that this Sabbath was a "high day."

"The Jews therefore, because it was the preparation, that the bodies should not remain upon the cross on the Sabbath day, **(for that Sabbath day was a high day,)** besought Pilate that their legs might be broken, and that they might be taken away."

Doesn't it make more sense to see that Christ was crucified on Thursday, the same afternoon the Passover lambs were being killed?

The next day which was called a "high day" was Friday, which was the High Sabbath referred to in John 19:31.

The regular Sabbath that week was on Saturday, as usual.

Jesus rode into Jerusalem on Sunday, which was the tenth day of the month. He was observed from Sunday until Thursday.

He was crucified late Thursday afternoon as the Passover lambs were being prepared and the blood was being smeared on the doorposts of their homes.

He was in the grave three days and three nights.

When Mary came to the tomb on Sunday morning, she came before sunrise (the seventeenth), and Jesus was already gone. We know He was raised on the 17th day of the month.

Summary

Sunday (10th) - Jesus rode into the city.

Monday (11th) - Jesus, the Lamb of God was observed.

Tuesday (12th) - Jesus, the Lamb of God was observed

Wednesday (13th) - Jesus, the Lamb of God was observed

Thursday (14th) - Late Thursday afternoon, Jesus, the Lamb of God was crucified. This was the same day the Passover lambs were being slain and their blood smeared on the doorposts of the homes.

Friday (15th) - This "Sabbath" was the High Sabbath John spoke of in John 19. Jesus was in the tomb.

Saturday (16th) - This was the regular Sabbath. Jesus was in the tomb.

Sunday (17th) - Jesus arose from the tomb sometime before sunrise on Sunday. Remember! According to the Jewish calendar, days were measured from sunset to sunset, not midnight to midnight, like we do.

The Importance of the 17th Day of the Month

Have you ever noticed how many important things took place on this very day, the 17th day of the month?

The flood came upon the world on the 17th day of the month.

The ark came to rest on Mt. Arafat on the 17th day of the month.

The Israelites crossed the Red Sea on the 17th day of the month.

The Israelites entered the Promised Land on the 17th day of the month.

The Lord gave Joshua instructions how to attack Jericho on the 17th day of the month.

Good King Hezekiah restored worship on the 17th day of the month.

After fasting 3 days, Queen Esther saved the Jews on the 17th day of the month.

The United Nations recognized Israel in 1948, on the 17th day of the month.

Mathematical Odds

Someone calculated that the odds of so many important events occurring on any given day are 1 chance in 783,864,876,960,000.000 that such events could take place.

From this alone it is clear that God controls the world and He watches over His people.

Isn't it wonderful to have a personal relationship with such a loving and powerful God who has promised heavenly dwellings for all who follow Him?

Chapter 5

Did Jesus Really Die for the World?

When Jesus Christ gave his life on the Cross of Calvary, who was Jesus really dying for?

Did Jesus die for the sins of the whole world? Or did He die for the elect and them alone?

There are two major views of the atonement. This is a very controversial subject and that is the focus of this chapter.

Limited Atonement

Those who believe Jesus died for the elect alone believe in a limited atonement. This view is also referred to as "particular redemption," because Jesus was dying "particularly" for the sins of the elect.

Unlimited Atonement

Those who believe that Jesus died for the sins of the whole world believe in an "unlimited Atonement."

The Atonement was unlimited in that the benefits of Christ's death were not limited to the elect but were realized by the whole world.

John Calvin (1509-1564)

There are three prominent theologians whose names come to mind when we consider the subject of the atonement. John Calvin was a French theologian who is best remembered for his teachings on the sovereignty of God, election, and predestination.

Jacobus Arminius (1560-1609)

Jacobus Arminius was a Dutch Calvinist who is the father of the system of theology known as "Arminianism.

Arminianism is a system of theology, formulated in the 17th century, which declares that human free will can exist without limiting God's power or contradicting the Bible.

Arminius believed that predestination was Biblical, and that God had intended some persons for heaven and others for hell, as indicated by Jesus' reference to "sheep and goats." But unlike John Calvin, Arminius focused more on God's love than on God's power.

Arminius believed in an unlimited atonement, but he did not believe in universal salvation or falling from grace. The belief that believers could "fall from grace" was added to Arminius' teachings after his death.

Moses Amyraldus (1569-1664)

Moses Amyraldus is believed to be the father of the Calvinists who believe in an unlimited atonement.

Prominent Calvinists of the Past

Prominent Calvinists of the past include: Arthur W. Pink (evangelist & scholar), Benjamin Keach (1689 Baptist Confession), Charles Spurgeon (Baptist preacher), George Whitefield (evangelist & preacher), George Whitefield (evangelist & preacher), John Calvin (preacher & Bible scholar), John Foxe (Foxe's Book of Martyrs),

John Gill (renowned theologian), John Knox (founder of Presbyterianism), Jonathan Edwards (evangelist), Martin Luther (Protestant Reformer), and Matthew Henry (Bible commentator).

Prominent Calvinists of the Present

Prominent Calvinists of the present include: R.C. Sproul and the popular Theological Seminary in Orlando, John Piper of Minneapolis, Mark Driscoll of Seattle, Albert Mohler of Southern Seminary, the ESV study Bible, the GENEVA study Bible, D.A. Carson, the late D. James Kennedy, James Montgomery Boice, James White, John F. MacArthur, and Martyn Lloyd-Jones.

Calvinist denominations include: Presbyterians, Primitive Baptists and the New Calvinists. The March 23, 2009 edition of TIME magazine has an article titled "The New Calvinism." It is a summary of who they are and what they teach.

Prominent Non-Calvinists

1. Universalists believe that Jesus died for the sins of the whole world. Universalists also believe that everyone in the world will eventually be saved.

2. Moderate Calvinists believe that Jesus died for the whole world, but they do not believe that everybody in the world will eventually be saved. Therefore, they are not "Universalist."

3. Four Point Calvinists, who believe in an unlimited atonement, but reject Universalism, are often referred to as Amyraldians, after Moses Amyraldius (1596-1664). These Calvinists are also referred to as "Four-Point" Calvinists because they believe four of the five points of Calvinism.

The "Five Points" of **Calvinism can be remembered by the** letters of the word "TULIP." Each letter in the word TULIP stands for a basic doctrine. Four-Point Calvinists reject the letter "L" which stands for "Limited Atonement."

4. Methodists, Pentecostals, Free-will Baptists and others who believe one can lose salvation are called Armenians. It is important to mention again that the belief that believers could "fall from grace" was added to Armenius's teachings after his death.

5. There are many Bible believing Christians who believe in eternal security, who are not Universalists, nor were ever a part of Rome or followers of John Calvin and his doctrines. For example, the Anabaptists were persecuted by the Catholic Church, by Luther, and by John Calvin. John Calvin said, "Anabaptist should be burned cruelly."

What does the Bible Teach?

There are Scripture verses which suggest that Jesus died for the elect. There are verses which suggest that Jesus died for the whole world. There are also verses which state that Jesus died for every man.

Let's look at each of these Scriptures and then you can arrive at your own conclusion.

Jesus died for the Elect

(Matthew 1:21) "And she shall bring forth a son, and thou shalt call his name JESUS: for he shall save his people from their sins."

(John 10:15) "As the Father knoweth me, even so know I the Father: and I lay down my life for the sheep."

(John 10:26-28) "But ye believe not, because ye are not of my sheep, as I said unto you. My sheep hear my voice, and I know them, and they follow me: And I give unto them eternal life; and they shall never perish, neither shall any man pluck them out of my hand."

(John 17:9) "I pray for them: I pray not for the world, but for them which thou hast given me; for they are thine."

(Acts 20:28) "Take heed therefore unto yourselves, and to all the flock, over which the Holy Ghost hath made you overseers, to feed the church of God, which he hath purchased with his own blood."

(II Tim. 1:9-10) "Who hath saved us, and called us with an holy calling, not according to our works, but according to his own purpose and grace, which was given us in Christ Jesus before the world began, But is now made manifest by the appearing of our Savior Jesus Christ, who hath abolished death, and hath brought life and immortality to light through the gospel"

(Ephesians 1:4) "According as he hath chosen us in him before the foundation of the world that we should be holy and without blame before him in love.

(Ephesians 5:25) "Husbands, love your wives, even as Christ also loved the church, and gave himself for it;"

(Revelation 13:8) "And all that dwell upon the earth shall worship him, whose names are not written in the book of life of the Lamb slain from the foundation of the world."

Jesus died for the world

(John 3:16) "For God so loved the world, that He gave his only begotten Son, that whosoever believeth in him should not perish, but have everlasting life. For God sent not his Son into the world to condemn the world; but that the world through him might be saved."

(John 1:29) "The next day John seeth Jesus coming unto him, and saith, Behold the Lamb of God, which taketh away the sin of the world."

(I John 2:2) "And he is the propitiation for our sins: and not for ours only, but also for the sins of the whole world."

Jesus died for all men

(Titus 2:11) "For the grace of God that bringeth salvation hath appeared to all men."

(1 Tim. 2:4) "Who will have all men to be saved, and to come unto the knowledge of the Truth.

(2 Peter 3:9) "The Lord is not slack concerning his promise, as some men count slackness; but is longsuffering to us-ward, not willing that any should perish, but that all should come to repentance."

Jesus paid a ransom for All

In these verses Paul states clearly that when Jesus died, His death paid a ransom for all.

(1 Tim. 2:6) "Who gave himself a ransom for all, to be testified in due time."

(1 Tim. 4:10) "For therefore we both labor and suffer reproach, because we trust in the living God, who is the Savior of all men, especially of those that believe.

Jesus even died for those who Deny Him

In II Peter 2:1, Peter reminds us that Jesus' death had even "bought" (died for) false teachers who were denying the Lord.

"But there were false prophets also among the people, even as there shall be false teachers among you, who privily shall bring in damnable heresies, even denying the Lord that bought them."

The word "bought" is from the Greek word "agorazo." The word "create" comes from the Greek word "ktizo." This verse says that Jesus bought them, not created them!

Jesus tasted death for Every Man

"But we see Jesus, who was made a little lower than the angels for the suffering of death, crowned with glory and honor; that he by the grace of God should taste death for every man (Hebrews 2:9).

Modern Calvinists Are Very Creative

Is it possible that Calvinists who are so aggressive in their efforts to convince others of a limited atonement are more interested in protecting a theological system than arriving at the plain truth?

In our honest opinion, the advocates of a limited atonement can become very creative when they are faced with the many scriptures that clearly teach that Christ died for the world. Please consider some specific examples of what we call "creative" interpretations.

Jesus died for all men: When advocates of a limited atonement read a verse that suggests that God desires all men to be saved and to come to a knowledge of the truth, **they interpret that one to mean** "God desires all men among the elect to be saved and come to the knowledge of the truth."

A ransom for all: When advocates of a limited atonement read verses that state that Jesus' death was a ransom for "all, *they interpret that to mean* Jesus gave his life a ransom *for* "all of the elect," or "all kinds of people among the elect."

The whole world: When it comes to verses that refer to the "whole world" advocates of a limited atonement interpret the word "world" in three different ways: Geographical, racial, and chronological. For example:

Geographical: They insist that the word "ours" in (I John 2:2) refers to the elect living in Asia Minor and the "whole world" refers to the elect living outside Asia Minor.

Racial: Advocates of a limited atonement tell us that "ours" means the elect from among the Jews, and the "whole world" refers to the elect among the Gentiles.

Chronological: Advocates of a limited atonement interpret "ours" to mean the elect living in the first century and "the whole world" to mean the elect living in later centuries.

Isn't this being creative?

What does the word "world" mean in the Bible?

It doesn't take a rocket scientist to understand what the word "world" means. Try this yourself. Get a concordance and read every Scripture where the word "world" is found, beginning in Matthew 4:8 and ending in Revelation 17:8. *See if you can find one reference where the word "world" refers to the elect.*

You will discover that references to the "world" mean just the opposite. Notice what the Bible says about the world that God loved, and Jesus died for.

Jesus died for that same world that hated Him. (John 7:7). "The world cannot hate you; but me it hateth, because I testify of it.

He died for that same world that hates Christians (John 15:18). "If the world hates you, ye know that it hated me before it hated you."

(John 17:14) "I have given them thy word; and the world hath hated them, because they are not of the world, even as I am not of the world."

(1 John 3:13) "Marvel not, my brethren, if the world hates you."

(John 15:19) "If ye were of the world, the world would love his own: but because ye are not of the world, but I have chosen you out of the world, therefore the world hateth you."

(John 12:31) "Now is the judgment of this world: now shall the prince of this world be cast out." Satan is the Prince of this world."

(John 14:30) "Hereafter I will not talk much with *you: for the prince of this world cometh, and hath nothing in me.*"

(I John. 2:15) Believers are not to love the world.

(1 John 2:2) "And He is the propitiation for our sins: and not for ours only, but also for the sins of the whole world."

Why Do People Go to Hell?

When lost people die and go to hell, do they go to hell because their sins were not covered by the death of Christ, or for some other reason? This is the question.

In our opinion, men and women go to hell, not because Christ did not die for them. They go to hell because they willfully reject the Gospel of Christ, who did die for them.

The Bible promises: "For whosoever calls upon the Name of the Lord shall be saved!" (Romans 10:13)

Jesus told us plainly why people go to hell in John 3:19: "And this is the condemnation. Light has come into the world, but men loved darkness rather than light because their deeds were evil."

Summary

Jesus died for the sins of the whole world. The Gospel is to be preached in the whole world. True Gospel preachers should be able to look people in the eye and tell them that God loves them, and that Christ died for them.

True Gospel preachers should look people in the eye and tell them they have a choice: They can accept Jesus and be saved or reject Jesus and spend eternity in hell.

True Gospel preachers should be able to conduct the funeral of a tiny baby and look the grieving parents in the eye and assure them that their child is not in hell.

Some pastors are preaching that some babies go to hell because God didn't love the child; or they are in hell because God decided to send the child to hell before the foundation of the world; or they are in hell because they were not baptized. This is not true.

True Gospel preachers should be able to look lost people in the eye anywhere in the world and tell them if they will repent and believe the Gospel, they will be saved.

Those who have put their trust in Jesus Christ should have the assurance of their salvation by believing the simple promises in the Word of God.

They should not fear that God may have damned them to hell before they were born. Nor should they depend on their infant baptism like John Calvin taught.

Each of us must decide where we stand on this issue. I want you all to know where I stand.

1. This present writer is not a Calvinist, an Arminian, or a Universalist. He is simply a Bible believing Christian.

2. This present writer does not accept the doctrines, books, or the teachings of the "Reform Theologians" or the "New Calvinists." The March 23, 2009 edition of **TIME** magazine has an article titled "The New Calvinism." This is the best summary of who they are and what they teach that we have seen recently.

3. Let us be more specific. This present writer does not accept the teachings of Loraine Boetner, R.C. Sproul, John Piper of Minneapolis, Mark Driscoll of Seattle, Albert Mohler of Southern Seminary, or the notes in the new Calvinist-flavored ESV study Bible, or the GENEVA study Bible.

4. In all honesty, this writer believes that those who really believe that Reform Theology or the New Calvinism is true would be more comfortable in Presbyterian or Primitive Baptist churches which have long believed and taught this doctrine.

We believe it is wrong to cause division and split other churches with this doctrine. In Proverbs 6, God clearly lists seven things that He hates.

One of the things God hates is "he who sows discord among the brethren."

This present writer predicts that the "New Calvinism" will divide churches and could possibly even destroy the Southern Baptist Convention.

Chapter 6

Did Jesus Really Rise from the Dead?

Did Jesus really rise from the dead or is the resurrection just a myth that has been handed down from generation to generation? This is a very important question. In fact, this is THE question. Why?

What if Jesus DID NOT RISE from the dead?

The resurrection of Christ is THE question, because the Bible itself admits that.

If Jesus did not rise from the dead, then Christianity is a hoax and preachers are lying to the people when they stand in the pulpits and preach the Gospel. Also, if the resurrection is not true, the bodies of Christians who died trusting in Christ to save them are rotting in their graves.

The Bible teaches this in I Corinthians 15:13-19.

13 But if there be no resurrection of the dead, then is Christ not risen:

14 And if Christ be not risen, then is our preaching vain, and your faith is also vain.

15 Yea, and we are found false witnesses of God; because we have testified of God that he raised up Christ: whom he raised not up, if so be that the dead rise not.

16 For if the dead rise not, then is not Christ raised:

17 And if Christ be not raised, your faith is vain; ye are yet in your sins.

18 Then they also which are fallen asleep in Christ are perished."

19 If in this life only we have hope in Christ, we are of all men most miserable."

What if Jesus DID RISE from the dead?

On the other hand, if Jesus did rise from the dead and if He is alive today, then:

1) Jesus is who He said He was, the Incarnate Son of God.

2) Jesus told the truth when He said that He was the ONLY WAY a person can know God, be saved, and get to heaven.

3) Those believers who died trusting in Christ to save them are with Him in heaven today.

4) And those who haven't repented of their sins and have not trusted in the finished work of Jesus on the cross are in deep trouble. They are lost and on their way to hell.

The Resurrection is the Foundation of Christianity

Christianity stands or falls on the fact of the Resurrection of Jesus Christ.

This present writer believes that God loved the world so much He sent His Son to die on the cross for our sins (John 3:16).

We believe Jesus died for the sins of the whole world.

We believe Jesus was in the grave for three whole days and three whole nights.

We believe Jesus came back to life on His own power on the First Day of the Week.

And finally, we believe that "Whoever shall call on the Name of the Lord shall be saved." (Romans 10:13)

Let's Examine the Historical Facts

Jesus rode into the city of Jerusalem on a donkey the Sunday before the day we call Easter. This happened on the tenth day of the month. We call this "Palm Sunday," because that was the day the people cut palm branches and placed them in the path of Jesus as he rode into the city. It is important to note that this was the fulfillment of one of the many prophecies that pointed to Christ as the Messiah.

On the tenth day of this month, the Jewish families would choose the lamb they would sacrifice for the Annual Passover and then observe the lamb until the fourteenth day to be sure it was without blemish and worthy to be offered as required in the Law of Moses.

That year, while the Jewish families were observing their lambs, without realizing what they were doing, they were also observing Jesus, the Lamb of God, who was going in and out of the city, teaching, preaching, and preparing to die for their sins.

Good Thursday: This writer believes in "Good Thursday" rather than "Good Friday." We believe that "Good Friday" is a tradition that is not supported by the facts. We believe Jesus died for our sins on Thursday (14th) of that week, on the very day the Passover lambs were being slain and their blood was being smeared on the door posts of each home with hyssop branches. This is the very day the Son of God (our Lamb of God) was being nailed to a cross for our sins.

Ram's horn: Every year, on this very day (14th), at 3:00 p.m. sharp, the Jewish High Priests would climb to the pinnacle of the temple and blow the ram's horn to signal that the Passover lambs had now been slain. On that day, although they did not know this at that time, the ram's horn was the signal to the people in the city that God's Son, the Lamb without blemish, had been chosen and was being slain for the sins of the world.

Wine and Myrrh: When people were being crucified, it was a merciful Jewish practice to give those led to execution a drink of strong wine mixed with myrrh as a "pain killer" to deaden their consciousness.

Hyssop branch: This mixture of sour wine was given on a branch of a hyssop plant. This was the very same bush the Jews used to apply the lamb's blood of the Passover Lamb to the doorposts of their homes. On that day the end of the hyssop stick pointed to the Lamb of God who was shedding His blood for their sins.

Darkness: The Bible says that there was darkness on the earth from noon until 3:00 p.m. A first century Greek historian named Thallus, who was not a Christian, wrote a history of the Eastern Mediterranean world in A.D. 52, and referred to this sudden darkness. He tried to explain this as a solar eclipse, though historical records show there was no normal eclipse on that date.

Buried: Jesus was taken down from the cross and placed in a borrowed tomb. The tomb was donated by a man named Joseph. After being placed in the borrowed tomb, Jesus was in that grave for three days and three whole nights. This was the "sign of Jonah" given by Jesus in Matthew 12:39-40.

Jesus arose from the dead: Sometime before sunrise on Sunday Morning, the 17th day of the month, Jesus came to life and came out of the tomb.

For the next forty days, Jesus appeared at least ten times and showed Himself to different groups and different people (Acts 1:3). Jesus appeared to couples in Luke 24:13. Jesus appeared to the disciples in John 20:19.

Jesus even appeared to five hundred people at one time (1 Corinthians 15:6). When the New Testament was written, most of those eye witnesses were still alive and could tell you what they had seen.

During that last appearance in view of 500 eye-witnesses, Jesus gave the promise of the Holy Spirit; sent his disciples into all the world to preach the Gospel; and promised to come again to receive us unto Himself.

God's plan of salvation

We cannot over-emphasize the importance of the resurrection of Christ. Other doctrines are important! This doctrine is essential. If the resurrection of Christ is not true, then Christianity is not true.

If the resurrection of Christ is not true, then the teachings of Christ and the death of Christ are of no value whatever.

If a person could successfully discredit the resurrection, then Christianity would fall like a house of cards. In addition to that, one must believe in the resurrection of Jesus Christ to be saved (I Corinthians 15:1-3).

1 "Moreover, brethren, I declare unto you the gospel which I preached unto you, which also ye have received, and wherein ye stand;

2 By which also ye are saved, if ye keep in memory what I preached unto you, unless ye have believed in vain.

3 For I delivered unto you first of all that which I also received, how that Christ died for our sins according to the scriptures;"

(Romans 10:9-13) "9 That if thou shalt confess with thy mouth the Lord Jesus, and shalt believe in thine heart that God hath raised him from the dead, thou shalt be saved.

10 For with the heart man believeth unto righteousness; and with the mouth confession is made unto salvation.

11 For the scripture saith, whosoever believeth on him shall not be ashamed.

12 For there is no difference between the Jew and the Greek: for the same Lord over all is rich unto all that call upon him.

13 For whosoever shall call upon the name of the Lord shall be saved."

Why do people reject the Gospel?

Some people may try to lead you to believe that they have rejected the Gospel because of intellectual or academic reasons. In my opinion, and according to the Bible, people reject the Gospel of Christ for moral reasons, not intellectual reasons.

The truth is, people reject the Gospel because they love their sins more than they love God and they cannot live in sin and be comfortable with the idea that there is a God who hates sin and will someday punish sin. Jesus made this clear in John 3:19-20.

" And this is the condemnation, that light is come into the world, and men loved darkness rather than light, because their deeds were evil. 20 For everyone that doeth evil hateth the light, neither cometh to the light, lest his deeds should be reproved."

A challenge for (honest) Skeptics

This present writer served in the ministry for more than half-a-century and has met very few honest skeptics with open minds. Most skeptics have spent little time examining the evidence for the Bible or the Gospel. They begin with the assumption that the Gospel is not true and then search for arguments to support their position.

Most of their time is spent reading the writings of other skeptics whose only true objective is to discredit the Gospel. These skeptics know all the answers but they 've not even heard the question.

We might add that some of the worst skeptics are apostate divinity students who attended liberal theological seminaries or state universities where they were never exposed to the hard evidence for the Bible or the Resurrection.

An honest skeptic must come to grips with the real issue which is this: What happened to the body of Christ? Honest skeptics will spend some time examining the real evidence for the Bible and the Gospel and then reach an intelligent conclusion.

History confirms that Jesus was crucified on a wooden cross.

History confirms the fact that Jesus was buried in a borrowed tomb. We know the name of the owner.

History confirms the fact that after three days and three nights the body of Jesus was missing.

The real question is: What happened to the body?

An honest skeptic must choose one of the following theories and base his/her life for now and eternity on that theory.

SIX POPULAR THEORIES

There are six possible theories as to the empty tomb and the missing body of Jesus. Each of us must "pick our seat and ride."

1. The Swoon theory

According to this theory, Jesus took a drug that made Him appear to die. When the cool air of the tomb revived Him, He emerged alive. No reputable scholars hold this view, but let's consider it.

Sweat Drops of Blood: The Bible says that, just before Jesus was arrested by the angry mob, when He was praying in the garden, a strange thing happened. (Luke 22:44) "And being in agony He prayed more earnestly: and his sweat was as it were great drops of blood falling down to the ground."

Hemohidrosis: The medical term sweating drops of blood is "hemohidrosis" or "hemahitrosis." This has been seen in patients who have experienced extreme stress or extreme shock to their systems. The capillaries around the sweat pores become fragile and leak blood into the sweat.

Beaten with Whips: Jesus was "flogged." Most people ignore this, but a doctor, by the name of C. Truman Davis, analyzed Roman beatings during the first century.

He concluded that Jesus must have been beaten to the edge of death. (Isaiah 52:13) "They shall see my Servant beaten and bloodied, so disfigured one would scarcely know it was a person standing there. So, shall He cleanse many nations."

Testimony of a Medical Doctor: Dr. Davis said: "Jesus was tied to a post and beaten thirty-nine times with a whip that had jagged bones and balls of lead woven into it.

The whip was brought down with full force upon his bare shoulders, back, and legs. At first the thongs cut through the skin.

Then, they cut deeper into the subcutaneous tissues, oozing blood from the capillaries and veins of the skin. Finally, those jagged bones and lead balls cut deeper until blood spurted from arteries and muscles.

The small balls of lead also produced deep bruises, broken open by subsequent blows. Eventually, the skin of the back hangs in long ribbons, an unrecognizable mass of torn, bleeding tissue.

Jesus Carried the Cross: After beaten to the point of death, Jesus was forced to carry his own cross 650 yards through a crowded street. His cross weighed between 80 and 110 pounds. Some have surmised that when He fell under that load, this may have led to a contusion of His heart, causing it to rupture on the cross.

Excruciating Pain: Do you know where the word "excruciating" came from? "Ex" means "out of" and "cruciate" means "to crucify." So brutal was the pain of crucifixion, the Romans coined a word to describe it. The word was "excruciating" meaning, "out of the cross."

The Nails: The nails used to crucify a man were 3/8 by 7 inches long. The wrists were considered part of the hands. The points of those nails would go into his wrists between the bones (so that no bones would be broken). These nails would go into the vicinity of the median nerve, causing shocks of pain to radiate through the victim's arms.

Another physician, Alex Metherell, who also extensively studied the crucifixion, is quoted in the Christian reader saying, this would cause agonizing pain akin to squeezing your funny bone with a pair of pliers.

The Wooden Cross: Standing at the crucifixion sites would be upright posts, called stipes, standing about seven feet high. On this main stipe was a crude seat. The part on which Jesus hands (wrists) were nailed was lifted and placed on the stipe.

His feet were then nailed to the stipes. To do this the knees had to be bent and the feet rotated laterally. (Psalm 22:14-17)

"14 I am poured out like water, and all my bones are out of joint: my heart is like wax; it is melted in the midst of my bowels."

15 My strength is dried up like a potsherd; and my tongue cleaveth to my jaws; and thou hast brought me into the dust of death.

16 For dogs have compassed me: the assembly of the wicked have enclosed me: they pierced my hands and my feet.

17 I may tell all my bones: they look and stare upon me."

Some of the best pictures on the details of death by crucifixion are available on the following website. They are based on a study by the Mayo Clinic. The next picture is a sample of what is available there.

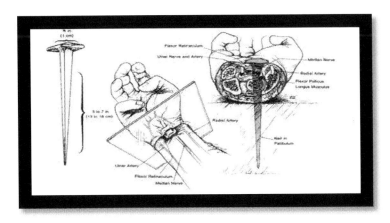

Consider these words from the Christian Reader:

"With his wrists and feet nailed securely, Jesus was hoisted into the air to hang. Because of the stress on his chest muscles, Jesus could inhale but could not exhale unless he pushed up with his feet to relieve the pressure.

If Roman executioners wanted to hasten death, they used a mallet to shatter the victim's shin bones, so he couldn't push up anymore. The victim's lungs would slowly fill with carbon dioxide, leading to asphyxiation.

The Romans did this to the two criminals crucified with Jesus. When they came to him, they saw he was already dead. To confirm that, a soldier thrust a spear between his ribs, puncturing the sac around his heart and the heart itself, causing a clear fluid and blood to drain out. Nobody survived the torment of the cross."

The article in the Christian Reader concluded: "Even if Jesus had not died on the cross and had revived in the tomb, think of the condition he would have been in when he appeared to his disciples. He wouldn't have prompted them to launch a world-wide movement on his behalf. They would have pitied him and rushed him to a doctor."

The Journal of American Medicine:

An article in the prestigious JAMA concluded: "Clearly, the weight of historical and medical evidence indicates that Jesus was dead before the wound in his side was inflicted. Accordingly, interpretations based on the assumption that Jesus did not die on the cross appear to be at odds with modern medical knowledge."

2. The Wrong Tomb:

Another theory was that the women went to the wrong tomb and found it empty. The truth is, we know where the real tomb was. We know the name of the owner. We also know that the tomb was heavily guarded, and a large stone covered the entrance to the tomb.

3. The disciples stole the body and then went out and lied about a resurrection that really didn't take place.

Testimony of Women: First, if the disciples made up the story, they would not have said that women discovered the empty tomb. In Jewish culture of that day, women had a low status and didn't qualify as legal witnesses.

The disciples would have said that some MEN discovered the grave empty. **Chuck Colson** was a special counsel to Richard Nixon during Watergate, and he saw how special conspiracies fall apart under pressure. Colson said:

"Is it really likely that a deliberate cover-up, a plot to perpetuate a lie about the Resurrection, could have survived the violent persecution of the apostles, the scrutiny of early church councils, the horrendous purge of first-century believers?"

4. The Jews or Romans stole the body.

Neither the Jews nor the Romans had reason to move the body. The Jews had Jesus killed and they wanted him to stay dead. If the Jews had stolen the body, don't you think they would have enjoyed parading it down the main street of Jerusalem, to silence the disciples, as they were preaching the resurrection on every corner?

5. Hallucination Theory:

Another theory is that the people who claimed to have seen Jesus alive after his crucifixion were hallucinating. **Gary Collins, president of the National Association of Psychologists**, says No! Collins said: "Hallucinations are individual events and cannot be shared between groups."

Collins also discounted the possibility of "group think," where a group of people encourage one another through the power of suggestion to see visions."

This Psychologist reminds us that the disciples were not anticipating a resurrection.

Testimony of another Doctor: Some people may not know, or they tend to forget that both the Gospel of Luke and the book of Acts were written by a medical doctor by the name of Luke. In Acts 1: 1-3 Doctor Luke wrote:

1"The former treatise have I made, O Theophilus, of all that Jesus began both to do and teach,

2 Until the day in which he was taken up, after that he through the Holy Ghost had given commandments unto the apostles whom he had chosen:

3 To whom also he showed himself alive after his passion by many infallible proofs, being seen of them forty days, and speaking of the things pertaining to the kingdom of God."

Testimony of the Apostle Peter: The apostle Peter, ran away from Jesus, denied Jesus, but later returned to Jesus and died as a martyr. History reminds us that Peter requested that he be crucified "upside down." Read what Peter said: (2 Peter 1:16-18).

16 "For we have not followed cunningly devised fables, when we made known unto you the power and coming of our Lord Jesus Christ but were eyewitnesses of his majesty.

17 For he received from God the Father honor and glory, when there came such a voice to him from the excellent glory, this is my beloved Son, in whom I am well pleased.

18 And this voice which came from heaven we heard, when we were with him in the holy mount."

Testimony of a former Terrorist

Another great piece of evidence for the resurrection is the conversion of the arch-enemy of the early church, Saul of Tarsus. He would be classified as a "terrorist" today.

Saul of Tarsus had dedicated his life to the destruction of the church. Then something happened! That terrorist was converted. This enemy of Christ claimed that Jesus had personally appeared to him and called him to preach. After that experience, that man spent the rest of his life preaching the faith he once tried to destroy. His ministry finally came to a climax when he was beheaded for his faith in the city of Rome.

Testimony of Skeptical Lawyer

The author of the article in the Christian Reader we have been quoting is Lee Strobel, a lawyer. Listen to what he said:

"Yale Law School trained me to be rational, and my years of sniffing for news at the Chicago Tribune had only toughened my cynical personality. But intrigued by changes in my wife after she became a Christian, I spent nearly two years studying evidence for the resurrection. I emerged convicted and gave my life to Christ. I have covered scores of criminal trials as a legal affairs journalist, and I never saw one with 515 witnesses."

6. Jesus literally arose from the grave (Romans 10:9-10)

"9 That if thou shalt confess with thy mouth the Lord Jesus, and shalt believe in thine heart that God hath raised him from the dead, thou shalt be saved.

10 For with the heart man believeth unto righteousness; and with the mouth confession is made unto salvation.

It is our prayer that you will believe in your heart that Jesus died for you and that you will confess this publicly with your mouth and become a true follower of Jesus Christ.

When you do, please send us an email: gk122532@gmail.com

Chapter 7

Is Jesus Really Coming Again?

The Second Coming of Jesus Christ is a fundamental teaching of the New Testament. We can read about the ascension of Christ in Acts 1:6-12.

6 When they therefore were come together, they asked of him, saying, Lord, wilt thou at this time restore again the kingdom to Israel?

7 And he said unto them, 'It is not for you to know the times or the seasons, which the Father hath put in his own power.

8 But ye shall receive power, after that the Holy Ghost is come upon you: and ye shall be witnesses unto me both in Jerusalem, and in all Judaea, and in Samaria, and unto the uttermost part of the earth.

9 And when he had spoken these things, while they beheld, he was taken up; and a cloud received him out of their sight.

10 And while they looked stedfastly toward heaven as he went up, behold, two men stood by them in white apparel;

11 Which also said, Ye men of Galilee, why stand ye gazing up into heaven? this same Jesus, which is taken up from you into heaven, shall so come in like manner as ye have seen him go into heaven.

12 Then returned they unto Jerusalem from the mount called Olivet, which is from Jerusalem a sabbath day's journey.

Read verse 11 again. 11 Which also said, Ye men of Galilee, why stand ye gazing up into heaven? this same Jesus, which is taken up from you into heaven, shall so come in like manner as ye have seen him go into heaven.

THREE IMPORTANT FACTS

There are three important facts revealed here that serve as the basis for our belief in the Second Coming of Jesus Christ.

1. Jesus is coming back to earth again.

2. His coming will be personal.

3. He will return to the earth in the same way He left the earth (This same Jesus . . . . shall so come in like manner as you have seen Him go into heaven.)

MUCH CONFUSION

This is just one of the many references to the Second Coming. But despite the clarity of this verse, there are many different interpretations of the Second Coming.

Preterism

Preterists believe Jesus returned in AD 70 when Titus and the Romans destroyed Jerusalem. They reject the idea of a future coming of Christ.

Pre-millennialism

Pre-millennialists believe Jesus will return for His church before the Tribulation and return with His church at the end of the Tribulation and will literally reign on the earth for one thousand years.

Mid Tribulation Rapture

Some believe Jesus will come for His church in the middle of the Tribulation, and like the Pre-Millennialists, they believe Jesus will reign on this earth for a literal one thousand years.

Post Tribulation Rapture

This group believes that the church will go through the Tribulation and Jesus will return for them at the end of this seven-year period and reign on the earth for one thousand years,

A-Millennialism

The "A" means "no!" A-Millennialists reject the entire idea of a literal one-thousand-year reign of Christ on the earth. They believe Jesus WILL return, raise all the dead, judge them, and eternity will begin.

Post Millennialism

Another group believes in the Second Coming and a Millennium, but they believe Jesus will return after (post) the Millennium.

Liberals

Most liberals do not believe in the inerrancy of the Scriptures, nor do many of them believe the Bible is the inspired Word of God. Most liberals interpret The Revelation allegorically, following the errors of Origen and the Alexandrian school and St. Augustine, the Roman Catholic Theologian.

Southern Baptist Moderates

Many (or most) of those pastors who call themselves "moderates" are A-millennialist. They reject the idea of a literal kingdom. They seldom preach from The Revelation or the Book of Daniel.

For example: They preach that the "Abomination of Desolation" was fulfilled when Antiochus IV polluted the temple by sacrificing a hog on the altar of the temple in 168-167 B.C. They preach that the tribulation scriptures in Matthew 24 and the Revelation were fulfilled at the destruction of Jerusalem by the Roman Titus in A.D. 70

Conservatives

There are many good conservatives who believe the Bible and take it literally but reject the idea of a "secret rapture." Some believe that the church will go through the Tribulation.

What should a serious Christian believe about the Second Coming of Jesus Christ? May I share my personal journey?

The Authors Personal Testimony

I was born in a Christian home, although I was not really saved until after I was married. My parents believed the Bible and my pastor attended the Moody Bible Institute and preached from a Scofield Bible. When I was saved and called to preach in 1953, I entered Stetson University and immediately came under the influence of liberals and soon rejected what my parents and pastor had taught me, and I became an A-Millennialist.

For more than fourteen years of my ministry, I preached a liberal Gospel. I denied the rapture, rejected the idea that anything in The Revelation was literal or for the future, nor would I have allowed myself to be caught with a Scofield Bible in my hand.

In 1967, just before accepting a call to become the pastor of the Cape Canaveral Baptist Mission, I returned to the faith of my parents and my pastor.

What about John Darby?

Opponents of the Rapture do have a strong argument. They maintain that the Rapture is a new doctrine and that nobody ever heard of it until John Darby, the Plymouth Brethren, and the Scofield Bible.

This is not true historically, but my answer to that argument is that "Justification by faith is a new doctrine. Nobody ever heard of it until Martin Luther and the protestant reformation."

Of course, both of those statements are false. I believe both doctrines were known and believed by the early church, but lost, and then re-discovered when men re-discovered the Scriptures.

THE SECOND COMING IS DIVIDED INTO TWO PARTS

We believe that the Second Coming of Christ is divided into two parts. He is coming FOR His people and then He is coming back WITH His people.

He is coming for His people BEFORE the Tribulation period.

He is coming back with His people AFTER the Tribulation.

When He comes for His people, He will come as a "thief in the night.

When He comes with His people, "every eye shall see Him."

When He comes for His people, we will meet Him "in the air."

When He comes back with His people, His feet will touch the earth and we will reign with Him 1000 years.

WHY WE BELIEVE IN A RAPTURE

The Outline of Revelation

Let us remind the reader again that we take The Revelation literally and we flatly reject the allegorical errors of Origen and the Alexandrian school of interpretation. We follow the teachings of the early church for the first three centuries. We believe The Revelation is divided into three sections.

Church Age (The Revelation 1-3):

The Tribulation (The Revelation 4-18),

The Consummation (The Revelation 19-22).

The church is not even mentioned anywhere in chapters 4-19. Why not? The reason is obvious. The church is no longer on earth in chapters 4-19.

The church was taken up in chapter four, verse 1. Read Revelation 4:1 again and take it literally. Where did the voice come from?

What did the voice (from heaven) tell John he was going to show him? It doesn't take a rocket scientist to understand this if you take it literally. The voice told John He was going to show John things that would take place "hereafter," or after the church age.

Chapter four follows chapter three. Those things would take place after chapter three. The church age is explained in chapters 2 and3. The things that the angel was going to show John would take place AFTER the church age and after the church is gone.

No Message to the Church

The second reason we believe in the Rapture is that that the chapters in the Gospel that describe the tribulation contain no warnings or message to the church. For example: In Matthew 24:15-20, we read about the *Abomination of desolation in the temple*. What temple? We meet in churches, not temples. Let those in Judea flee to mountains?

What if we live in Gainesville or Jacksonville? Do we flee to Georgia?

Pray that your flight is not on the Sabbath? Do Christians have any problem traveling on Saturday?

Not only is the church not mentioned in chapters 4-18 (in The Revelation), there is no message for the church in the Scriptures explaining the Tribulation.

The Purpose of the Tribulation

There are two reasons why God is sending the Tribulation on the earth, and neither of them have any meaning for the church.

The first purpose of the Tribulation is to prepare Israel for the coming of her Messiah.

The second purpose of the Tribulation is to punish this God-hating, Christ-rejecting, sin-loving world (Revelation 16:4-6). The church will not go through the Tribulation.

Illustrations from the Old Testament

A fourth reason we believe the church will be raptured before the Tribulation is because of the "types" in the Old Testament. A "type" is something in the Old Testament that illustrates some great truth in the New Testament.

Joseph was a "type" of Christ. I believe the presence of God's people on earth keep the Tribulation from beginning. I also believe the moment we are gone; the Tribulation will begin.

For example: When God sent angels to destroy Sodom and Gomorrah, they told Lot they could not destroy Sodom until they had led Lot safely outside the city (Genesis 19:21) and (2 Peter 2:5-9).

God protected Noah when He sent the flood to destroy the earth and every living thing.

God protected Rahab the harlot when He sent Joshua to destroy the city of Jericho.

God will protect His people from the coming Tribulation.

We Are in Good Company

It is important for every reader to understand that every major evangelist and conservative Christian writer since 1900 has held the Pre-millennial view.

Among them are men like: Evangelist Billy Sunday, Frank Norris, Hyman Appleman, Bob Jones Sr., Dr. M.R. DeHann, Dr. John R. Rice, Evangelist Billy Graham, Dallas Billington, Jack Wertzon, Jack Van Impe, Dr. Lee Roberson, Dr. John R. Rice, Jack Wertzon, Jack Van Impe, R. G. Lee, Dr. Adrian Rogers, Tim Lahaye, Dr. Dwight Pentecost, Dr. John Walvoord, Dr. Charles E. Fuller, and many others.

EIGHT FACTS ABOUT THE RAPTURE

1. There will be no "signs" to warn us of the Rapture.

There are plenty of signs to tell us the Second Coming is near. Read Matthew4:29. There are *NO* signs to tell us the rapture is near (1 Thessalonians 5:1-9).

2. Jesus Will Come for Us.

In John 14:1-4 Jesus gave His word that He would come back for us. Death is not His coming. Pentecost was not His coming. Conversion is not His coming. Jesus is coming for us.

3. Jesus Will Come Personally.

Death is not the Second Coming. Pentecost was not the Second Coming. Jesus did not return PERSONALLY in AD 70. The same Jesus who was seen going up in Acts 1 will personally return for His people (1 Thessalonians 4:16). "The Lord Himself will come, but He will not touch the earth. We will meet Him "in the air." (1 Thessalonians 4:17).

4. There Will Be a Shout.

He will probably shout a command (1 Thessalonians 4:16). It will be like Jesus calling Lazarus out of the tomb (John 11:43). The dead will hear His voice (John 5:28). The world will hear thunder, the saints will hear His voice (John 12:28) & (Acts 9:7).

5. There Will Be a Trumpet Blast (1 Thessalonians 4:16).

God used the trumpet to assemble His people in the Old Testament. This will be the final assembly. I Corinthians 15:52 calls this the "last" trumpet. When was the first trumpet? (Exodus 19:13) (Hebrews 12:26).

6. Dead Christians will be Raised & Translated (changed into their heavenly bodies). (See 1 Thessalonians 4:16) The Christians who have died will rise before those who are still alive at that time.

7. Living Saints will be Translated without dying (1 Thessalonians 4:17). There will be life on earth "as usual" when this happens. Some people will never die.

8. There is no "Partial Rapture."

Some teach a "partial" Rapture where Jesus takes only those who are spirit filled and living right at that moment. When Jesus comes for His Bride, He will take her whole body, not just her arms or legs. Consider the illustrations of this in the Old Testament.

Lot represents carnal Christians. God spared Lot even though he was carnal.

Enoch represents "Spirit filled" Christians. Both were "taken" to safety. When Christ comes, He will take ALL His people safely home.

ARE YOU READY?

Jesus could return for His people at any time. Will you be going with us or will you be left behind? There will be people saved after the Rapture but most of them will probably die as martyrs. (Revelation 6:9-11).

9 And when he had opened the fifth seal, I saw under the altar the souls of them that were slain for the word of God, and for the testimony which they held:

10And they cried with a loud voice, saying, how long, O Lord, holy and true, dost thou not judge and avenge our blood on them that dwell on the earth?

11And white robes were given unto every one of them; and it was said unto them, that they should rest yet for a little season, until their fellow-servants also and their brethren, that should be killed as they were, should be fulfilled."

These are men and women who died for their faith during the Tribulation and are pleading with God to judge their persecutors on earth, who are still living and killing believers.

These people are dead, but they have not been resurrected yet. This also means that they were not part of the church because the church has already been raptured and the "dead in Christ" who were raised from their graves and had been given resurrection bodies at the Rapture.

Others may survive by hiding out in caves and away from the cities. We know there will be a great multitude saved because we read about them in The Revelation. They are said to have come out of the Great Tribulation. In our opinion, they will more than likely be those who have never heard the Gospel, or who had heard it and rejected it.

(Revelation 7:9-17) 9After this I beheld, and, lo, a great multitude, which no man could number, of all nations, and kindreds, and people, and tongues, stood before the throne, and before the Lamb, clothed with white robes, and palms in their hands;

10And cried with a loud voice, saying, Salvation to our God which sitteth upon the throne, and unto the Lamb.

[11]And all the angels stood round about the throne, and about the elders and the four beasts, and fell before the throne on their faces, and worshipped God, Saying, Amen: Blessing, and glory, and wisdom, and thanksgiving, and honor, and power, and might, be unto our God for ever and ever. Amen.

[13]And one of the elders answered, saying unto me, what are these which are arrayed in white robes? and whence came they?

[14]And I said unto him, Sir, thou knowest. And he said to me, these are they which came out of great tribulation, and have washed their robes, and made them white in the blood of the Lamb.

[15]Therefore are they before the throne of God and serve him day and night in his temple: and he that sitteth on the throne shall dwell among them.

[16]They shall hunger no more, neither thirst anymore; neither shall the sun light on them, nor any heat.

[17]For the Lamb which is in the midst of the throne shall feed them and shall lead them unto living fountains of waters: and God shall wipe away all tears from their eyes."

How Will They Hear the Gospel?

They will hear the Gospel from one of three sources during the Great Tribulation.

There will be 144,000 Jewish witnesses preaching.

There will be two witnesses who preach, are killed, and return to life (seen around the world on the internet and TV), and.

Finally, God will send an angel flying over the land preaching the "everlasting Gospel."

Chapter 8

Will Jesus Really Reign on Earth for 1,000 Years?

A careful study of the Old Testament reveals that there are two lines of prophecy pointing to the coming of Christ into the world. Those two lines of prophecy are very different. They are so different it caused some people to wonder if Jesus was really the promised Messiah.

We are aware that many who read this will not agree, but we believe that Jesus will return to earth and literally reign on this earth for one thousand years. Then and only then, will there be peace on earth. One cannot read the Scriptures and not notice the many references to the kingdom.

The Importance of the Kingdom

The first question the wise men asked when they arrived in Jerusalem was, "Where is he that is born King of the Jews? (Matthew 2:1-2).

The first sermon John the Baptist preached was about the Kingdom (Matthew 3:10).

The first sermon Jesus preached was about the Kingdom (Matthew 4:17).

When giving the Lord's Prayer, Jesus told His disciples to pray, "Thy Kingdom come."

When Jesus spoke with Nicodemus, He told him he had to be born again to enter the Kingdom (John 3)

The last question the disciples asked Jesus before He ascended into heaven was, "Wilt thou at this time restore the KINGDOM to Israel?" (Acts 1:6-7)

The last sermon Paul preached was about the Kingdom (Acts 28:30).

WHY IS THERE SO MUCH CONFUSION?

Why is there so much confusion over the concept of the kingdom? What caused all the confusion? People became confused because Jesus did not do everything the prophets said the Messiah would do the first time He came.

Are There Two Messiahs?

Some even wondered if there were supposed to be two Messiahs. They had read the prophecies that predicted the Messiah would come as a suffering servant.

They had also read the predictions of Messiah setting up a kingdom, delivering Israel from her enemies, and sitting on David's throne as king. When Jesus didn't set up His earthly Kingdom, they were confused. Jesus came the first time to die for our sins.

What they failed to understand was that the Messiah would come twice. Jesus would come the first time to suffer and die for our sins.

He will come the second time to set up His kingdom and reign as King over all the earth for 1000 years.

The Second Coming of Christ is both literal and personal. Read Acts 1:8-11. The same Jesus who ascended into heaven will return the same way (*in like manner as ye have seen Him go into heaven*).

1. Death is not the Second Coming

In John 14, Jesus said He was going away to prepare a place for us and when it was ready He would come again and receive us unto Himself. Some teach that this means when we die Jesus comes to get us and take us home. Death is not the Second Coming.

2. Pentecost was not the Second Coming

Some teach that the Second Coming was fulfilled when the Holy Spirit came upon the disciples and the church was born. This is not the Second Coming.

3. Conversion is not the Second Coming.

Others teach that when a person is saved, Jesus comes to them and begins to live His life through them. Conversion is not the Second Coming.

4. The Rapture is not the Second Coming.

Now we understand that most liberals reject the idea of the Rapture. We don't.

We believe Jesus will come FOR His people before the Great Tribulation and He will come WITH His people after the Tribulation.

There are no SIGNS prior to the Rapture. Jesus will come without warning and snatch His bride away.

The world will not see Him when He comes in the Rapture. He will come like a "thief in the night."

His Second Coming will be totally different. There are all kinds of "signs" for the Second Coming. Read Matthew 24, Luke 21, and Mark 13.

When Jesus comes the second time, at the end of the Tribulation, every eye will see Him and all the tribes on the earth will mourn.

The Rapture will be in secret and there are no signs given. We are simply told to be ready.

The Second Coming, in contrast will be no secret. Everybody on earth will see Him when He comes.

"Behold, He is coming with clouds and every eye shall see Him, even they who pierced Him. And all the tribes of the earth shall mourn because of Him." (Revelation 1:7)

THREE VIEWS OF THE KINGDOM

1. A Literal Kingdom

The first view of the kingdom is that the kingdom will be a literal, visible, one-thousand-year, earthly reign of Jesus Christ on this earth. This was the position of all the prophets of the Old Testament and the position of the disciples and the early church. This is our position.

2. Spiritual Kingdom

The second view is that The Kingdom of God is the rule and reign of Jesus Christ in the heart of the believer. Those who believe in a spiritual kingdom believe that since Jesus didn't set up a kingdom and reign, those prophecies were not to be taken literally. They totally reject the idea of Jesus coming back and reigning on this earth in a literal kingdom of 1000 years. This is a very popular position.

3. The Kingdom is the Church

The third view is that the kingdom is the church. This is the position of the Roman Catholic Church. Although this idea originated with the Catholics, there are many non-Catholics who share this view as well.

Don't confuse Israel with the church. This position is often referred to as "Replacement Theology." In other words, the church has replaced Israel as God's chosen people.

This position has several different branches, but their reasoning goes something like this. When the Jews as a nation rejected Jesus, God canceled all those promises, and anything related to the future of Israel, now applies to the church, or is not to be taken literally. Be careful here.

This is not sound doctrine. Israel is Israel and the church is the church. God has a plan for both in the latter days.

Read Romans 11. Jesus is the literal Messiah. He came literally the first time to die for our sins.

He will come again literally to fulfill all those prophecies, set up His kingdom, sit on a literal throne in Jerusalem, and rule for a literal 1000 years.

TWELVE FACTS ABOUT THE COMING KINGDOM

1. Jesus will return to earth in power (Revelation 19:11-15)

"11 And I saw heaven opened and behold a white horse; and he that sat upon him was called Faithful and True, and in righteousness he doth judge and make war.

12 His eyes were as a flame of fire, and on his head were many crowns; and he had a name written, that no man knew, but he himself.

13 And he was clothed with a vesture dipped in blood: and his name is called The Word of God.

14 And the armies which were in heaven followed him upon white horses, clothed in fine linen, white and clean.

15 And out of his mouth goeth a sharp sword, that with it he should smite the nations: and he shall rule them with a rod of iron: and he treadeth the winepress of the fierceness and wrath of Almighty God."

2. Satan will be bound for 1,000 years (Revelation 20:1-3).

1 "And I saw an angel come down from heaven, having the key of the bottomless pit and a great chain in his hand.

2 And he laid hold on the dragon, that old serpent, which is the Devil, and Satan, and bound him a thousand years,

3 and cast him into the bottomless pit, and shut him up, and set a seal upon him, that he should deceive the nations no more, till the thousand years should be fulfilled: and after that he must be loosed a little season."

3. Believers will reign on this earth (Revelation 20:4).

"And I saw thrones, and they sat upon them, and judgment was given unto them: and I saw the souls of them that were beheaded for the witness of Jesus, and for the word of God, and which had not worshiped the beast, neither his image, neither had received his mark upon their foreheads, or in their hands; and they lived and reigned with Christ a thousand years."

4. Wild animals will be tame (Isaiah 11:6-8).

"The wolf also shall dwell with the lamb, and the leopard shall lie down with the kid; and the calf and the young lion and the fatling together; and a little child shall lead them.

7. And the cow and the bear shall feed; their young ones shall lie down together: and the lion shall eat straw like the ox.

8. And the sucking child shall play on the hole of the asp, and the weaned child shall put his hand on the cockatrice' den."

5. Christians will judge the world (I Corinthians 6:1-3).

1 "Dare any of you, having a matter against another, go to law before the unjust, and not before the saints?

2 Do ye not know that the saints shall judge the world? And if the world shall be judged by you, are ye unworthy to judge the smallest matters?

3 Know ye not that we shall judge angels? How much more things that pertain to this life?"

6. Jesus Christ will end all war and bring peace (Isaiah 2:4).

"And He shall judge among the nations and shall rebuke many people: and they shall beat their swords into plowshares, and their spears into pruning-hooks: nation shall not lift up sword against nation, neither shall they learn war anymore."

(Micah 4:3-4) 3 "And he shall judge among many people, and rebuke strong nations afar off; and they shall beat their swords into plowshares, and their spears into pruning hooks: nation shall not lift up a sword against nation, neither shall they learn war any more.

4 But they shall sit every man under his vine and under his fig tree; and none shall make them afraid: for the mouth of the Lord of hosts hath spoken it."

7. Jesus Christ will rule as king over all the earth (Zechariah. 14:8-9)

8 "And it shall be in that day, that living waters shall go out from Jerusalem; half of them toward the former sea, and half of them toward the hinder sea: in summer and in winter shall it be.

9 And the LORD shall be king over all the earth: In that day shall there be one LORD."

8. There will be a perfect environment.

Al Gore will be happy. For the first time in history, the entire earth will be in balance. There has never been a time so far when the world has had a chance to see God, man, animal life, vegetable life, and the environment, all living in perfect harmony. During the millennium, man will have a chance to see what life would have been like on earth if sin had not entered and corrupted Gods' creation.

9. There will be universal health care (Isaiah 35: 5-6)

5 "Then the eyes of the blind shall be opened, and the ears of the deaf shall be unstopped.

6 Then shall the lame man leap as a hart, and the tongue of the dumb sing: for in the wilderness shall waters break out, and streams in the desert."

10. People will live longer (Isaiah 65:20)

"There shall be no more thence an infant of days, nor an old man that hath not filled his days: for the child shall die a hundred years old."

11. God will open the eyes of the Jews (Zechariah 12:7-10).

7 The Lord also shall save the tents of Judah first, that the glory of the house of David and the glory of the inhabitants of Jerusalem do not magnify themselves against Judah.

8 In that day shall the Lord defend the inhabitants of Jerusalem; and he that is feeble among them at that day shall be as David; and the house of David shall be as God, as the angel of the Lord before them.

9 And it shall come to pass in that day, that I will seek to destroy all the nations that come against Jerusalem.

10 And I will pour upon the house of David, and upon the inhabitants of Jerusalem, the spirit of grace and of supplications: and they shall look upon me whom they have pierced, and they shall mourn for him, as one mourneth for his only son, and shall be in bitterness for him, as one that is in bitterness for his firstborn.

12. The Citizens of the Kingdom.

The resurrected Saints of the New Testament will be there. The resurrected Saints of the Old Testament will be there. One third of the Jews in Israel who survive the Great Tribulation will be there (Zechariah 13:8-9). And the martyrs from the Tribulation will be there.

WHEN WILL JESUS ESTABLISH HIS KINGDOM?

Believers in every generation have looked for Christ to return in their lifetime. This has been going on for two thousand years now. Is Jesus really coming back or are we confused?

If you want to know when Jesus is coming back to set up His kingdom, read the second chapter of Daniel. The king had a dream that troubled him. There were two problems. He couldn't remember what he dreamed, nor neither did he know the meaning of the dream.

God gave Daniel a divine revelation which enabled Daniel to explain the dream and the interpretation. The story is recorded in Daniel 2:24-45).

24 Then Daniel went in to see Arioch, whom the king had ordered to execute the wise men of Babylon. Daniel said to him, "Don't kill the wise men. Take me to the king, and I will tell him the meaning of his dream."

25 Arioch quickly took Daniel to the king and said, "I have found one of the captives from Judah who will tell the king the meaning of his dream!"

26 The king said to Daniel (also known as Belteshazzar), "Is this true? Can you tell me what my dream was and what it means?

27 Daniel replied, "There are no wise men, enchanters, magicians, or fortune-tellers who can reveal the king's secret.

28 But there is a God in heaven who reveals secrets, and he has shown King Nebuchadnezzar what will happen in the future. Now I will tell you your dream and the visions you saw as you lay on your bed.

29 "While Your Majesty was sleeping, you dreamed about coming events. He who reveals secrets has shown you what is going to happen. And it is not because I am wiser than anyone else that I know the secret of your dream, but because God wants you to understand what was in your heart.

31 In your vision, Your Majesty, you saw standing before you a huge, shining statue of a man. It was a frightening sight.

32 The head of the statue was made of fine gold. Its chest and arms were silver, its belly and thighs were bronze, 33 its legs were iron, and its feet were a combination of iron and baked clay.

34 As you watched, a rock was cut from a mountain, but not by human hands. It struck the feet of iron and clay, smashing them to bits.

35 The whole statue was crushed into small pieces of iron, clay, bronze, silver, and gold. Then the wind blew them away without a trace, like chaff on a threshing floor. But the rock that knocked the statue down became a great mountain that covered the whole earth.

36"That was the dream. Now we will tell the king what it means.

37 Your Majesty, you are the greatest of kings. The God of heaven has given you sovereignty, power, strength, and honor.

38 He has made you the ruler over all the inhabited world and has put even the wild animals and birds under your control. You are the head of gold.

39 "But after your kingdom comes to an end, another kingdom, inferior to yours, will rise to take your place. After that kingdom has fallen, yet a third kingdom, represented by bronze, will rise to rule the world.

40 Following that kingdom, there will be a fourth one, as strong as iron. That kingdom will smash and crush all previous empires, just as iron smashes and crushes everything it strikes.

41 The feet and toes you saw were a combination of iron and baked clay, showing that this kingdom will be divided. Like iron mixed with clay, it will have some of the strength of iron.

42 But while some parts of it will be as strong as iron, other parts will be as weak as clay.

43 This mixture of iron and clay also shows that these kingdoms will try to strengthen themselves by forming alliances with each other through intermarriage. But they will not hold together, just as iron and clay do not mix.

44 "During the reigns of those kings, the God of heaven will set up a kingdom that will never be destroyed or conquered. It will crush all these kingdoms into nothingness, and it will stand forever.

45 That is the meaning of the rock cut from the mountain, though not by human hands, that crushed to pieces the statue of iron, bronze, clay, silver, and gold. The great God was showing the king what will happen in the future. The dream is true, and its meaning is certain."

This is a preview of every world power from Babylon to the coming of Christ to set up His Kingdom

In this vision, God revealed to Daniel every world power from the time of Babylon until the coming of Jesus Christ to set up His Kingdom.

The Babylonian came first, followed by the kingdom of the Medes and the Persians (arms of silver). This was followed by the Greek empire under Alexander (the belly and thighs of brass). The two legs of iron were the Eastern and Western divisions of the Roman Empire.

Now, follow this carefully

Following the Roman Empire (legs of iron), there will be ten "kings" (European leaders) represented by the feet of iron and clay. This is important.

These feet on the image came from the same geographical region (Europe) of the ancient Roman Empire.

The Bible makes it clear that there will never be another empire as strong as the legs of iron. Notice this union is illustrated by iron mixed with clay, which usually doesn't happen. In the dream, a stone was cut from the mountains. This stone is Jesus Christ.

Notice Where the Stone Hit the Image

The stone hit the image in the feet. Notice we said "feet." Those ten toes are ten kings. Daniel 2:44 says: "During the reigns of those kings, the God of Heaven will set up a kingdom that will never be destroyed or conquered. It will crush all these kingdoms into nothingness, and it will stand forever."

Jesus did not return and set up His kingdom in the days of the Babylonians.

Jesus did not return and set up His kingdom in the days of the Persian Empire.

Jesus did not return and set up His kingdom in the days of the Greek Empire.

Neither did Jesus return and set up His kingdom in the days of the Roman Empire.

The Stone Hit the Image in its Feet.

The Bible says that in the days of those ten kings Jesus will return to earth, put an end to all earthly kingdoms, and set up his perfect kingdom on this earth.

This has not happened yet. This is still future. Now, I am going to speculate here. Could these ten "kings" be the leaders of ten European nations? We can't be dogmatic, but it's not hard to imagine the European Union being the foundation for this confederation.

The Coming One World Government

The Bible predicts that in the end times, there will be a one world government and a one world (false) religion. This unholy union is pictured in The Revelation as a harlot riding on the back of a beast. The harlot represents the false religion and the beast represents the one-world government.

A Woman Riding a Beast

Go on the internet and go to Google images. Type in "woman riding a beast" and see what you find there. You will see a statue of a woman riding a beast standing at this moment in front of the European Union Building in Brussels Belgium.

Next, type in Euro-dollar and look at the picture. In my opinion, it's later than we think. Prophecy is being fulfilled before our very eyes.

Summary

Will there ever be peace on earth? When? There will be peace on this earth when Christ returns *WITH* His people and reigns with them (us) on this earth for one thousand years.

When will this happen? It will happen seven (7) years after He returns to earth FOR His people.

Jesus could return to earth FOR His people anytime. There are no more "signs" to be fulfilled.

When Jesus returns and takes His people out of this world (the Rapture) the earth will endure seven (7) years of tribulation.

During that time, there will be one world government and a one world false religion (I believe will be Islam).

This unholy alliance is pictured in chapter 17 of The Revelation as a woman (the harlot) riding the beast. The harlot is the apostate religion and the beast is the one world government.

The Bible says (see Daniel 2 again) that in the days of those kings (10 nation federation), The God of heaven will set us a kingdom that will never be destroyed. Read Daniel 2 again. Jesus is the stone that hits the image in its feet. It doesn't take a rocket scientist to figure this out. All we must do is to read the Bible and believe it.

There is only one way to enter God's Kingdom. To enter God's Kingdom, you must repent of your sins, believe that Jesus Christ died for your sins and rose again, and receive Jesus Christ as your Savior. If you will do that, you will be "born again!" That's a promise. Here is a suggested Prayer.

Dear God,
I admit that I have sinned.
I'm sorry that I have sinned.
I believe you died for me and are alive today.
Today, I am willing to repent of my sins and
ask you to come into my heart.
Please forgive my sins and save my soul.
I ask this in the Name of Jesus,
Amen.
May God bless you,
Gene Keith
gk122532@gmail.com

Chapter 9

Did Jesus Believe in a Literal Heaven?

When was the last time you heard a sermon or read a book about heaven? Were most of your questions answered in that sermon or book? Could you answer the following questions about heaven if someone asked you?

1. Where is heaven?

2. Is heaven a real place or is it a spiritual state?

3. Do people go to heaven immediately after they die, or do they pass through purgatory first?

4. Will we know each other in heaven?

5. Can people in heaven see what's going on down here on earth? If they can see us down here, how can there not be tears in heaven?

6. Will we have bodies in heaven or will we just be spirits?
The Bible teaches that heaven is a wonderful place and our finite minds cannot comprehend the amazing things God has prepared for those who love Him.

"But as it is written, Eye hath not seen, nor ear heard, neither have entered into the heart of man, the things which God hath prepared for them that love him. 10 But God hath revealed them unto us by his Spirit: for the Spirit searcheth all things, yea, the deep things of God (I Corinthians 2:9-10).

In the following pages of this book we will try to answer some of the most common questions people ask about heaven.

1. Is heaven a literal place?

Heaven is not some *make believe place* in the clouds where angels in night gowns play harps all day long. *Heaven is just as real as Gainesville, Jacksonville, or Atlanta.* In fact, some have joked about people dying and having to go through Atlanta to get to heaven, just like most airlines go through Atlanta on their way to most other cities.

Jesus said that heaven was a real place (John 14:1-6). "Let not your heart be troubled: ye believe in God, believe also in me.

2 In my Father's house are many mansions: if it were not so, I would have told you. I go to prepare a place for you.

3 And if I go and prepare a place for you, I will come again, and receive you unto myself; that where I am, there ye may be also.

4 And whither I go ye know, and the way ye know.

5 Thomas saith unto him, Lord, we know not whither thou goest; and how can we know the way?

6 Jesus saith unto him, I am the way, the truth, and the life: no man cometh unto the Father, but by me."

2. How many heavens are there?

The first heaven is the sky just above the earth where birds and airplanes fly (Genesis 1:20). "And God said, Let the waters bring forth abundantly the moving creature that hath life, and fowl that may fly above the earth in the open firmament of heaven."

The second heaven is outer space where the moon, the sun, and other planets are (Psalm 19:1-2). "The heavens tell of the glory of God. The skies display his marvelous craftsmanship. 2 Day after day they continue to speak; night after night they make him known."

There is also a place called the third heaven. Paul claimed to have been there (2 Corinthians 12:1-4). Consider what the Apostle said about an experience he had. It may have been one of those "out of body" experiences. We are not sure. Neither was he. Read what he said.

"This boasting is all so foolish but let me go on. Let me tell about the visions and revelations I received from the Lord.

2 I was caught up into the third heaven fourteen years ago.

3 Whether my body was there or just my spirit, I don't know; only God knows.

4 But I do know that I was caught up into paradise and heard things so astounding that they cannot be told."

There are a lot of popular books out there today in which people described their visit to heaven or hell. You are welcome to your opinion about those experiences, and I have mine.

Those books sell well, and the authors have made a lot of money. But I go back to the experience Paul had (described above) and you will notice that he was not allowed to tell of the things he saw or heard.

Why was Paul not allowed to tell of those experiences and authors today can tell of them and make loads of money? *Just asking*.

Anyway, the third heaven is where people go when they die. This isn't purgatory, but it is a temporary place while we wait for the new heavens and the new earth described in The Revelation. This is where the thief on the cross with Jesus went when he died. Jesus told him, *"Today, you will be with me in paradise."*

There will be a new heaven and a new earth someday (Revelation 21:1-5).

"Then I saw a new heaven and a new earth, for the old heaven and the old earth had disappeared. And the sea was also gone.

2 And I saw the holy city, the New Jerusalem, coming down from God out of heaven like a beautiful bride prepared for her husband.

3 I heard a loud shout from the throne, saying, "Look, the home of God is now among his people! He will live with them, and they will be his people. God himself will be with them.

4 He will remove all of their sorrows, and there will be no more death or sorrow or crying or pain. For the old world and its evils are gone forever."

5 And the one sitting on the throne said, 'Look, I am making all things new!" And then he said to me, write this down, for what I tell you is trustworthy and true."

3. Where is heaven?

If you were to ask the average person where heaven was they would say "up." If you asked them to point toward heaven, they would point "up." The truth is, wherever we are on this planet and point up, we are really pointing "out."

Heaven is not out. Heaven is up, and there is only one direction that is literally up and that is north! The Bible teaches that heaven is NORTH.

Consider the following Scriptures

(Isaiah 14:12-14) How art thou fallen from heaven, O Lucifer, son of the morning? How art thou cut down to the ground, which didst weaken the nations?

13 For thou hast said in thine heart, I will ascend into heaven, I will exalt my throne above the stars of God: I will sit also upon the mount of the congregation, **in the sides of the north:**

14 I will ascend above the heights of the clouds; I will be like the most High."

(Psalm 48:2) "Beautiful for situation, the joy of the whole earth, is mount Zion, on the **sides of the north**, the city of the great King."

The earth is tilted exactly 23.5 degrees and the axis of the earth is pointed directly toward the North Star (Polaris). We are not saying that Polaris is heaven, but we are saying that the only direction that is "UP" from the earth is "NORTH." So, where is heaven? As far as we know, *heaven is north from the earth.*

4. How big is heaven?

By far, the best sermon this present writer ever heard on heaven was preached by *Evangelist Danny Lanier.* In that message, Danny mentioned things about heaven we had never heard before. The information below is from Danny's sermon.

It is important for you to remember that the statistics you are about to read refer to the new heaven and the new earth described in Revelation 21, *not the present heaven* (paradise) where believers are now.

1500 square miles: To get an idea of how large the ground floor of heaven is, we could begin at Miami, Florida and draw a line 1,500 miles to the north to the State of Maine.

From Maine we would draw the line 1,500 miles westward to Denver, Colorado. From Denver, we would draw the line south to somewhere in Mexico. Finally, we would draw the line eastward, across the Gulf of Mexico until we reached our point of departure. *That square would be heaven's base.*

528,000 Stories: Heaven is also 1,500 miles high. Our space stations and satellites orbit a mere 250 miles above the earth at 17,000 mph. Heaven's "top floor" will be 1,250 miles higher than our space stations.

We measure the heights of buildings by the number of floors. The World Trade Center had more than 100 floors.

If each floor of heaven would have 15-foot ceilings (rather than the normal 8-foot ceilings), heaven would have 528,000 stories and each story would have 2,250,000 square miles (not feet) of space on every floor. That's 1 trillion, 188 billion square miles of space in God's city.

386,000 square miles for each person: It is estimated that 30 billion people have been born on earth since creation. If all of them died and went to heaven (which we know they won't), each of them would have 198 square miles of space in heaven.

If only half of the people ever born went to heaven, they would each have 396,000 square miles of space in heaven.

5. Do we go to heaven immediately when we die?

Jesus told a true story which is recorded in Luke 16:19-31 about two men who died. One went straight to heaven and the other went straight to hell. This is a true story, not a parable. Jesus even gave us the name of the beggar who died and went to heaven. His name was Lazarus.

This, by the way, is not the Lazarus mentioned in John 11 whom Jesus raised from the dead. Both men Jesus talked about in Luke 16 lived at the same time, lived in the same town, and walked the same streets.

(Luke 16:19-31)19 "There was a certain rich man who was clothed in purple and fine linen and fared sumptuously every day.

20 But there was a certain beggar named Lazarus, full of sores, who was laid at his gate,

21 desiring to be fed with the crumbs which fell from the rich man's table. Moreover, the dogs came and licked his sores.

22 So it was that the beggar died and was carried by the angels to Abraham's bosom. The rich man also died and was buried.

23 And being in torments in Hades, he lifted up his eyes and saw Abraham afar off, and Lazarus in his bosom.

24 "Then he cried and said, 'Father Abraham, have mercy on me, and send Lazarus that he may dip the tip of his finger in water and cool my tongue; for I am tormented in this flame.'

25 But Abraham said, 'Son, remember that in your lifetime you received your good things, and likewise Lazarus evil things; but now he is comforted, and you are tormented.

26 And besides all this, between us and you there is a great gulf fixed, so that those who want to pass from here to you cannot, nor can those from there pass to us.'

27 "Then he said, 'I beg you therefore, father, that you would send him to my father's house,

28 for I have five brothers, that he may testify to them, lest they also come to this place of torment.'

29 Abraham said to him, 'They have Moses and the prophets; let them hear them.'

30 And he said, 'No, father Abraham; but if one goes to them from the dead, they will repent.'

31 But he said to him, 'If they do not hear Moses and the prophets, neither will they be persuaded though one rise from the dead.'"

Both men died and were buried. But here's where strange things begin to happen. They went in different directions. The beggar went immediately to heaven and the rich man went immediately to hell. *"And it came to pass, that the beggar died, and was carried by the angels into Abraham's bosom."* (Verse 22) This poor beggar was carried by the angels.

What were the angels carrying?

Where were they carrying it? They weren't carrying his body, for his body was put in a dumpster or buried somewhere in the landfill. **The angels were carrying** the beggar's spirit. He went directly to heaven.

Our bodies are compared to tents (2 Corinthians 5:1-10)

1 For we know that when this earthly tent we live in is taken down (that is, when we die and leave this earthly body), we will have a house in heaven, an eternal body made for us by God himself and not by human hands.

2 We grow weary in our present bodies, and we long to put on our heavenly bodies like new clothing.

3 For we will put on heavenly bodies; we will not be spirits without bodies.

4 While we live in these earthly bodies, we groan and sigh, but it's not that we want to die and get rid of these bodies that clothe us. Rather, we want to put on our new bodies so that these dying bodies will be swallowed up by life.

5 God himself has prepared us for this, and as a guarantee he has given us his Holy Spirit.

6 So we are always confident, even though we know that as long as we live in these bodies we are not at home with the Lord.

7 For we live by believing and not by seeing.

8 Yes, we are fully confident, and we would rather be away from these earthly bodies, for then we will be at home with the Lord.

9 So whether we are here in this body or away from this body, our goal is to please him.

10 For we must all stand before Christ to be judged. We will each receive whatever we deserve for the good or evil we have done in this earthly body.

When saved people die, they go immediately to heaven. When the beggar died, his sufferings were over. He was home at last. That's where saved people go when they die. There is no purgatory. There is no soul sleep. When we die, it is heaven or hell forever. But there's more.

We go to heaven immediately and we leave our "tents" (or our earth-suits, which are our mortal bodies) in a closet called a cemetery.

But one day, we are coming back for our clothes (I Thessalonians 5:13-18). Christ will return, raise our bodies, put us back in them, and we will wear our new bodies for 1000 years here on earth before we enter the final heaven described in Revelation 21.

(Thessalonians 4:13-18) 13 And now, brothers and sisters, I want you to know what will happen to the Christians who have died so you will not be full of sorrow like people who have no hope.

14 For since we believe that Jesus died and was raised to life again, we also believe that when Jesus comes, God will bring back with Jesus all the Christians who have died.

15 I can tell you this directly from the Lord: We who are still living when the Lord returns will not rise to meet him ahead of those who are in their graves.

16 For the Lord Himself will come down from heaven with a commanding shout, with the call of the archangel, and with the trumpet call of God. First, all the Christians who have died will rise from their graves.

17 Then, together with them, we who are still alive and remain on the earth will be caught up in the clouds to meet the Lord in the air and remain with him forever."

18 So comfort and encourage each other with these words.

Stephen saw heaven opened just before he died. (Acts 7:56-60). "56 And he told them, "Look, I see the heavens opened and the Son of Man standing in the place of honor at God's right hand!"

57 Then they put their hands over their ears, and drowning out his voice with their shouts, they rushed at him.

58 They dragged him out of the city and began to stone him. The official witnesses took off their coats and laid them at the feet of a young man named Saul.

59 And as they stoned him, Stephen prayed, "Lord Jesus, receive my spirit."

60 And he fell to his knees, shouting, "Lord, don't charge them with this sin!" And with that, he died."

Paul wanted to die and go on to heaven (Philippians 1:23-24).

"I'm torn between two desires: Sometimes I want to live, and sometimes I long to go and be with Christ. That would be far better for me, 24 but it is better for you that I live."

Yes, when saved people die, they go immediately to heaven.

6. Will we know each other in heaven?

The following picture is of my great-grandson, Landen. His mother, Charity and his father, Steven, are seen holding him in her arms. The sad part is, she didn't get to hold Landan very long, because little Landan died in just four days. We believe with all our hearts, we will see little Landan again. What do we base this hope on? Read the story of David and his child who lived only seven days.

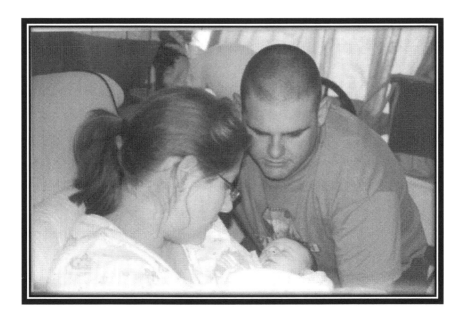

I believe we will know each other in heaven. We will be able to see Landan, talk with Landan, and Tuelah will finally get to hold him (although he probably won't be a baby when we get there).

David believed that he would see his son who died in infancy (2 Samuel 12:18-23).

18 Then on the seventh day the baby died. David's advisers were afraid to tell him. "He was so broken up about the baby being sick," they said. "What will he do to himself when we tell him the child is dead?"

19 But when David saw them whispering, he realized what had happened. "Is the baby dead?" he asked."Yes," they replied.

20 Then David got up from the ground, washed himself, put on lotions, and changed his clothes. Then he went to the Tabernacle and worshiped the LORD. After that, he returned to the palace and ate.

21 His advisers were amazed. "We don't understand you," they told him. "While the baby was still living, you wept and refused to eat. But now that the baby is dead, you have stopped your mourning and are eating again."

22 David replied, "I fasted and wept while the child was alive, for I said, 'Perhaps the LORD will be gracious to me and let the child live.'

23 But why should I fast when he is dead? Can I bring him back again? I will go to him one day, but he cannot return to me."

Jesus said that we would sit down with Abraham, Isaac, and Jacob (Matthew 8:11). "And I tell you this, that many Gentiles will come from all over the world and sit down with Abraham, Isaac, and Jacob at the feast in the Kingdom of Heaven."

The disciples recognized Moses and Elijah on the Mount of Transfiguration (Matthew 17:1-6). "Six days later Jesus took Peter and the two brothers, James and John, and led them up a high mountain.

2 As the men watched, Jesus' appearance changed so that his face shone like the sun, and his clothing became dazzling white.

3 Suddenly, Moses and Elijah appeared and began talking with Jesus.

4 Peter blurted out, "Lord, this is wonderful! If you want me to, I'll make three shrines, one for you, one for Moses, and one for Elijah."

5 But even as he said it, a bright cloud came over them, and a voice from the cloud said, "This is my beloved Son, and I am fully pleased with him. Listen to him."

6 The disciples were terrified and fell face down on the ground.."

Paul told us we will be with our loved ones again in the presence of the Lord (1 Thessalonians 4:13-18).

"13 But I do not want you to be ignorant, brethren, concerning those who have fallen asleep, lest you sorrow as others who have no hope.

14 For if we believe that Jesus died and rose again, even so God will bring with Him those who sleep in Jesus.

15 For this we say to you by the word of the Lord, that we who are alive and remain until the coming of the Lord will by no means precede those who are asleep.

16 For the Lord Himself will descend from heaven with a shout, with the voice of an archangel, and with the trumpet of God. And the dead in Christ will rise first.

17 Then we who are alive and remain shall be caught up together with them in the clouds to meet the Lord in the air. And thus, we shall always be with the Lord.

18 Therefore comfort one another with these words.

7. What will heaven be like?

We don't have as much information on this as we would like to have but we have "glimpses" here and there.

"But as it is written, Eye hath not seen, nor ear heard, neither have entered into the heart of man, the things which God hath prepared for them that love him. 10 But God hath revealed them unto us by his Spirit: for the Spirit searcheth all things, yea, the deep things of God" (I Cor. 2:9-10).

Heaven will be much better than anything that exists on this earth. So, think about the most beautiful scenery, the most beautiful homes, and the most enjoyable places there are on this earth. Believe me, heaven will be better than that. There are some beautiful homes and places on earth, but heaven will be better than any of these.

8. Can people in heaven see us down here on earth?

In my opinion they can see us. Jesus said there is joy in the presence of the angels in heaven when one sinner is saved (read Luke 15).

If there is joy in the presence of the saved people in heaven, the people in heaven must have some way of knowing what's going on down here on the earth.

If there is joy, isn't it reasonable that there will also be sorrow (in the present heaven)? "Wherefore seeing we also are compassed about with so great a cloud of witnesses, let us lay aside every weight, and the sin which doth so easily beset us, and let us run with patience the race that is set before us." (Hebrews 12:1)

Who are these witnesses? Those witnesses are the very people *mentioned by name* in Hebrews 11:1-40). They served God faithfully in their generation and now they are like the alumni sitting in the grandstands. They are watching us and cheering us on. They must also weep when they see us fall.

9. Are there tears in the present heaven?

How can there be *no tears* in heaven when we can see what's happening down here and all our friends who aren't saved? In our opinion, there will be a lot of tears and sorrow in heaven until the time God wipes always all tears from our eyes and creates the new heaven and new earth (Revelation 21:4-5).

When that time comes, God will erase the memory of this earth, this life, and everything associated with it (Isaiah 65:17). "For, behold, I create new heavens and a new earth: and the former shall not be remembered, nor come into mind."

Somewhere between now and the new heaven and earth, Jesus will deal with His children (2 Corinthians 5:10). I personally believe Jesus will judge believers following the Rapture (Revelation 4:1). We will be judged for our works during that seven years when the earth is going through the Great Tribulation.

When Christ removes His church, the earth will enter the Tribulation period (Revelation 4-19).

During that seven-year period, while the earth is going through the Tribulation, we believers will be standing before the BEMA Judgment Seat of Christ and judged for our works (2 Corinthians 5:10) (I Corinthians 3).

It is during that period that Christ will deal with rebellious, disobedient Christians as seen in Luke 12:43-48. This will take place after we leave this earth and before God creates the new heaven and new earth.

43 Blessed is that servant, whom his lord when he cometh shall find so doing.

44 Of a truth I say unto you, that he will make him ruler over all that he hath.

45 But and if that servant says in his heart, my lord delayeth his coming; and shall begin to beat the menservants and maidens, and to eat and drink, and to be drunken;

46 The lord of that servant will come in a day when he looketh not for him, and at an hour when he is not aware, and will cut him in sunder, and will appoint him his portion with the unbelievers.

47 And that servant, which knew his lord's will, and prepared not himself, neither did according to his will, shall be beaten with many stripes.

48 But he that knew not, and did commit things worthy of stripes, shall be beaten with few stripes. For unto whomsoever much is given, of him shall be much required: and to whom men have committed much, of him they will ask the more.

In the final heaven there will be no sorrow, crying, tears, sickness, death, etc., for the former things will have passed away. Serious thinking people will be preparing for the future.

Both Saved and lost will someday stand before God to be judged, but they won't both appear at the same time or in the same judgment.

Saved people will be judged at the BEMA Seat of Christ (2 Corinthians 5:10).

Unsaved people will appear before the Great White Throne (Revelation. 20:11-15).

10. Will you be in heaven?

I served as Pastor in local churches from 1954 until 2010 and from my personal experience, I am convinced that our churches today are filled with people who have never been born again.

The tragedy is, many of those people don't realize they are lost. Now, I can read your mind. Some of you are saying, *"Pastor Gene! You are judging!"* You're right. I am judging. The Bible says: "By their fruit you will know them."

People who are really saved don't continue to live in sin (I John 3)

"Behold, what manner of love the Father hath bestowed upon us, that we should be called the sons of God: therefore, the world knoweth us not, because it knew him not.

2 Beloved, now are we the sons of God, and it doth not yet appear what we shall be, but we know that, when he shall appear , we shall be like him; for we shall see him as he is .

3 And every man that hath this hope in him purifieth himself, even as he is pure.

4 Whosoever committeth sin transgresseth also the law: for sin is the transgression of the law.

5 And ye know that he was manifested to take away our sins; and in him is no sin.

6 Whosoever abideth in him sinneth not: whosoever sinneth hath not seen him, neither known him.

7 Little children let no man deceive you: he that doeth righteousness is righteous, even as he is righteous.

8 He that committeth sin is of the devil; for the devil sinneth from the beginning. For this purpose, the Son of God was manifested, that he might destroy the works of the devil.

9 Whosoever is born of God doth not commit sin; for his seed remaineth in him: and he cannot sin, because he is born of God.

10 In this the children of God are manifest, and the children of the devil: whosoever doeth not righteousness is not of God, neither he that loveth not his brother."

Saved people are changed people (2 Corinthians 5:17). "Therefore, if any man be in Christ, he is a new creature: old things are passed away; behold, all things are become new."

Some people won't know they are not going to heaven until it is too late (Matthew 7:21-27). 21 "Not everyone that saith unto me, Lord, Lord, shall enter into the kingdom of heaven; but he that doeth the will of my Father which is in heaven.

22 Many will say to me in that day, Lord, Lord, have we not prophesied in thy name? and in thy name have cast out devils? and in thy name done many wonderful works?

23 And then will I profess unto them, I never knew you: depart from me, ye that work iniquity.

24 Therefore whosoever heareth these sayings of mine, and doeth them, I will liken him unto a wise man, which built his house upon a rock:

25 And the rain descended, and the floods came, and the winds blew, and beat upon that house; and it fell not: for it was founded upon a rock.

26 And everyone that heareth these sayings of mine, and doeth them not, shall be likened unto a foolish man, which built his house upon the sand:

27 And the rain descended, and the floods came, and the winds blew, and beat upon that house; and it fell: and great was the fall of it."

Chapter 10

Did Jesus Believe in a Literal Hell?

There are four different words in the Bible that are translated "hell" in the English language. However, they'd don't always refer to the same place.

The Hebrew word Sheol

This is the word that is translated hell throughout the Old Testament. This word does not describe the final abode of lost sinners. It often refers to the grave.

The Greek word Hades

This literally means *the realm of the dead*. This is the realm of disembodied spirits. When people die, both saved and lost enter "hades" or the realm of the dead.

Both paradise and torment are in the realm of the dead. Those who are saved enter paradise. Those who are lost enter torment (see Luke 16).

The Greek word Tartarus

This word is used in 2 Peter 2:4 and it describes the place where the angels who sinned are kept in prison until the final judgment. "For if God did not spare the angels who sinned, but cast them down to hell (tartarus) and delivered them into chains of darkness, to be reserved for judgment."

The Greek word Gehenna

This is the word which describes the place where lost sinners will spend eternity. This is final hell or the lake of fire. This is the word Jesus used when He warned us to cut off our hands and pluck out our eyes if they were causing us to sin. He said we would be better off without hands or eyes if that would keep us out of *Gehenna.*

This is also the place we read about in The Revelation 20:11-14, where sinners are cast after being judged at the Great White Throne Judgment. God will call the dead out of Hades and their bodies out of their graves. When He is finished, death and the present hell will be cast into the lake if fire. This is called the second death (Revelation 20:11-14).

"11 Then I saw a great white throne and Him who sat on it, from whose face the earth and the heaven fled away. And there was found no place for them.

12 And I saw the dead, small and great, standing before God, and books were opened. And another book was opened, which is the Book of Life. And the dead were judged according to their works, by the things which were written in the books.

13 The sea gave up the dead who were in it, and Death and Hades delivered up the dead who were in them. And they were judged, each one according to his works.

14 Then Death and Hades were cast into the lake of fire. This is the second death.

It is interesting to note that hell was not made for man. Hell was designed as a place to punish the Devil and his angels. But men and women will go there as well when they sin and reject the free gift of salvation Jesus provided when He died on the cross. Now, let's consider the six facts about hell Jesus revealed to us in Luke 16.

1. People in hell can still see with their eyes (Luke 16:23).

"And in hell he lift up his eyes, being in torments, and seeth Abraham afar off, and Lazarus in his bosom."

2. Jesus said that people in hell can still talk with their mouths (Luke 16:24).

"And he cried and said, Father Abraham, have mercy on me, and send Lazarus, that he may dip the tip of his finger *in water, and cool my tongue; for I am tormented in this flame."*

3. Jesus said that people in hell can still feel pain (Luke 16: 24b).

". . . .and send Lazarus, that he may dip the tip of his finger in water and cool my tongue; for I am tormented in this flame."

4. Jesus said that people in hell can still hear with their ears and remember with their minds (Luke 16: 25-26).

"But Abraham said, Son, remember that thou in thy lifetime receivedst thy good things, and likewise Lazarus evil things: but now he is comforted, and thou art tormented.

26 And beside all this, between us and you there is a great gulf fixed: so that they which would pass from hence to you cannot; neither can they pass to us, that would come from thence."

5. Jesus taught that people in hell can still pray (Luke 16:27-31).

27 Then he said, I pray thee therefore, father, that thou wouldest send him to my father's house: 28 For I have five brethren; that he may testify unto them, lest they also come into this place of torment.

29 Abraham saith unto him, They have Moses and the prophets; let them hear them. 30 And he said, Nay, father Abraham: but if one went unto them from the dead, they will repent. 31 And he said unto him, if they hear not Moses and the prophets, neither will they be persuaded, though one rose from the dead."

Hell is Serious Business

Jesus went to a lot of trouble to warn you that there is a heaven to gain and a hell to shun. Hear his warning again: "And in hell he lifted up his eyes, being in torments." (Luke 16:23)

In the story that Jesus told in Luke 16, you will notice that once the man entered hell there was no way out.

He couldn't have any water. He could not go across to where Abraham and Lazarus were. Abraham and Lazarus certainly didn't want to go across to where he was. We plead with you in the Name of Jesus, to repent of your sins and accept the gift of salvation Jesus provided for you when He died on the cross.

Chapter 11

Did Jesus Really Believe the Bible?

It is becoming increasingly common today to meet people who say they believe in Jesus but do not accept the Bible as the inspired Word of God.

Christians Should Believe What Jesus Believed

In our opinion, if you are a serious follower of Jesus Christ, you will believe what Jesus believed about the Bible. Jesus believed the Bible. For those who claim to be Christians yet look upon the stories of the Bible as allegorical, let us remind you that Jesus took those stories literally.

1.   Jesus Believed in Creation, Adam and Eve (Matthew 19:4-6)

⁴ And he answered and said unto them, have ye not read, that he which <u>made them</u> at the beginning made them male and female,

⁵ And said, for this cause shall a man leave father and mother, and shall cleave to his wife: and they twain shall be one flesh?

⁶ Wherefore they are no more twain, but one flesh. What therefore God hath joined together, let not man put asunder.

2. Jesus Believed in Noah and the Flood (Matthew 24:36-39)

36 But of that day and hour knoweth no man, no, not the angels of heaven, but my Father only.

37 But as the days of Noah were, so shall also the coming of the Son of man be.

38 For as in the days that were before the flood they were eating and drinking, marrying and giving in marriage, until the day that Noe entered into the ark,

39 And knew not until the flood came, and took them all away; so, shall also the coming of the Son of man be.

3. Jesus believed the Story of Sodom and Gomorrah (Luke 17:28-29)

28 Likewise also as it was in the days of Lot; they did eat, they drank, they bought, they sold, they planted, they builded;

29 But the same day that Lot went out of Sodom it rained fire and brimstone from heaven and destroyed them all.

4. Jesus Believed in Jonah was swallowed by a Great Fish (Matthew 12:38-40)

38 Then some of the scribes and Pharisees answered, saying, Teacher, we want to see a sign from you.

39 But He answered and said to them, "An evil and adulterous generation seeks after a sign, and no sign will be given to it except the sign of the prophet Jonah.

40 For as Jonah was three days and three nights in the belly of the great fish, so will the Son of Man be three days and three nights in the heart of the earth."

40 For as Jonah was three days and three nights in the belly of the great fish, so will the Son of Man be three days and three nights in the heart of the earth."

The miracle of Jonah as not that Jonah remained alive in the belly of the whale for three days and three nights. The miracle is that he died in the belly of the whale. He was dead three days and three nights and God brought him back to life and sent him on to Nineveh to preach.

The REAL miracle was that Jonah came out the same way he went in (through the whale's mouth).

5.   Jesus Said the Holy Spirit Would Reveal the Future to His Disciples (John 16:12-14)

[12] I have yet many things to say unto you, but ye cannot bear them now. [13] Howbeit when he, the Spirit of truth, is come, he will guide you into all truth: for he shall not speak of himself; but whatsoever he shall hear, that shall he speak: **and he will show you things to come**. [14] He shall glorify me: for he shall receive of mine and shall show it unto you.

Summary

Jesus believed the Bible. In our opinion, if you are a serious follower of Jesus Christ, you will believe what Jesus believed about the Bible. We also encourage you to find a church where the pastor believes that the Bible is the inspired Word of God.

Read your Bible. Believe your Bible. Follow your Bible.

Chapter 12

What Do You Believe About Jesus?

Who is This Person Called Jesus?

Was Jesus Really Born of a Virgin?

Was Jesus Really Born on Christmas Day?

Was Jesus Really Crucified on Good Friday?

Did Jesus Really Die for the Whole World?

Did Jesus Really Rise from the Dead?

Is Jesus Really Coming Back Again?

Will Jesus Literally Reign as King over the Earth?

Did Jesus Really Believe in Heaven?

Did Jesus Believe in Hell?

Did Jesus Really Believe the Bible?

One Solitary Life

"He was born in an obscure village, the child of a peasant woman. He grew up in still another village, where He worked in a carpenter shop until He was 30. Then for three years He was an itinerant preacher.

He never wrote a book. He never held an office. He never had a family or owned a house. He didn't go to college. He never traveled more than 200 miles from the place He was born. He did none of the things one usually associates with greatness. He had no credentials but Himself.

He was only 33 when public opinion turned against Him. His friends deserted Him. He was turned over to His enemies and went through the mockery of a trial. He was nailed to a cross between two thieves. When He was dying, His executioners gambled for His clothing, the only property He had on earth. When He was dead, He was laid in a borrowed grave through the pity of a friend.

Nineteen centuries have come and gone, and today He is the central figure of the human race, the leader of mankind's progress. All the armies that ever marched, all the navies that ever sailed, all the parliaments that ever sat, all the kings that ever reigned, put together, have not affected the life of man on earth as much as that One Solitary Life. Do You Know Who He Is?"

by Dr. James Allan Francis

An Invitation

Would you like to become a true follower of Jesus Christ? If you are willing to repent of your sins and believe the Gospel, you can be saved right now, wherever you are while you are reading this. To repent of your sins means that you are sorry for your sins and you are willing to turn from them.

Would you like to have your sins forgiven and be saved? If so, pray the following prayer from your heart. Why not do it right now? The following is a suggested prayer.

Dear God,

I know that I am sinner.

I believe that you died for me and you are alive today.

Right now, Jesus, I want to turn from my sins and be saved.

Please forgive me. Come into my heart and save me.

I will do my best to live for you from now until the day I die.

In Jesus' Name,

Amen.

Name_____ Date _____

Witness _____ Date _____

About the Author

Gene Keith was born William Eugene Keith in Tarpon Springs, Florida, on December 25, 1932. His parents were Walter Keith Jr. Louise (Campbell) Keith. He graduated from Tarpon Springs High School in 1950, and married his sweetheart, Tuelah Evelyn Riviere in 1952. Tuelah's parents were Lawrence and Viola Riviere. Gene became Christian in 1952 and entered the ministry in 1953.

Florida Baptist Witness

The following material is from "**Circling the Wagons**," which appeared in the Florida Baptist Witness January 28, 2013 Joni B. Hannigan, Managing Editor).

Gene Keith is part of a ten-generation legacy of pioneer Christian leaders from Kentucky, Texas, and Florida. Since 1773 when John Keith hosted the first meeting of Virginia's Ten Mile Baptist Church, the Keith men for at least ten generations have led their congregations as Baptist preachers, elders or deacons, to be pioneers in sharing the Gospel.

By wagon, on horseback, on foot, and by car, they've traveled carrying the Good News of Christ from the thick forests of Virginia, across the green mountains of Kentucky, to the High Plains of Texas before finally turning back southeast to settle in sun-drenched Central Florida where three generations now pastor two churches just 20 miles apart. "

Communications

Gene has many years of experience in broadcasting, not only as a "DJ," but including his own daily talk show type program known as "The Sound of Inspiration," which was popular on several radio stations in North Central Florida. He had an afternoon show on the first FM Country Music station in Gainesville.

Education

Gene attended Stetson University, the University of Florida, and received his BA from Luther Rice College. He has many years of experience in the Christian School movement. He is the founder of the Countryside Christian School which celebrated its 42nd Anniversary in 2016. He has experience as a pastor and a Christian School Principal.

Gene also served as a *Consultant Field Representative* for *Accelerated Christian Education*, during which time he helped establish several Christian Schools in Florida. Many of his family are involved in education serving as Principals and teachers.

Politics

Gene also has experience in the political arena. He has run for the office in State Senator, The Florida House of Representatives, and the United States Congress. In one election, he lost by one *percentage point* (499 votes).

Travel

Gene has traveled to many of the popular places including England, France, Germany, Italy, Greece, and especially Israel. Gene spent a week in Israel immediately following the Six-Day War in 1967.

Retired Pastor

Gene has served as pastor in Taft, Otter Creek, and the Pastor of the First Baptist Church of Cape Canaveral, Florida in 1968-1969, when America sent the first astronauts to the moon. He served as the pastor of the Southside Baptist Church of Gainesville twice. Gene retired after 50 plus years in the ministry and is presently Pastor Emeritus of the Countryside Baptist Church of Gainesville, Florida. Gene turned 85 on Christmas Day 2017 and spends most of his time writing and speaking.

Published Author

Gene has more than twenty books already available and several in the process. His books are available from Amazon, both in Kindle format and in print.

Other Books by Gene Keith

You Can Understand the Revelation.
Daniel: The Key to Prophecy
Cremation: Are You Sure?
Religious but Lost
Suicide: Is Suicide the Unpardonable Sin?
Getting Started Right: A Handbook for Serious Christians
Easter: Facts versus Fiction
How to Enjoy Christmas in a World that has lost its Way
Evolution: Facts versus Fiction
Why do Bad Things Happen to God's People?
The Radical Same Sex Revolution
Can a Saved Person Ever be Lost Again?
Otter Creek: True Stories of People and Places
Public School or Christian School?
One Nation Under God - or Allah. Can America Survive?
Financial Solutions (A Handbook for Church Leaders)
Our Story: God is Good- - All the Time!
Stop Changing History
The Pope, Peter, Walls, Guns, and Donald Trump
10 Serious Issues Christians Must Face
The Gifts of the Holy Spirit & Speaking in Tongues
The Midnight Cry

If you would like to order any of Gene's books, go to Amazon.com and type in Gene Keith Books, or the title of the book you desire and simply follow the links. You may also correspond with Gene by email: **gk122532@gmail.com.**

Made in the USA
Columbia, SC
01 November 2023

24888517R00074